# A Step By Step Guide
## SQL Server 2012
## With Management Studio 2012

### By
### Neal Gupta
MCP, MCAD, MCSD, SCJP

**Books by Neal:**

*30 Minutes Step By Step Guide Team Foundation Server 2010 for Visual Studio 2010*

*30 Minutes Step By Guide Team Foundation Server (TFS) 2010 With TFS Azure (Cloud)*

*A Step By Step Guide to SQL Server 2012 with Management Studio 2012*

# Table of Contents:

## *Chapter 1: Introduction*

SQL Server 2012 is a **R**elational **D**atabase **M**anagement **S**ystem (RDMS) that is used to manage data that is stored in various tables in a relational way. This data can be as simple as customers' details containing first name, last name, and address specifics or as complicated as hundreds of tables. SQL Server 2012, being a RDBMS, lets you to create, update, delete, or search a specific or all of the customers' information, as you want, in an efficient way [using a language called SQL/T-SQL, we will discuss more about it in later chapters]. Moreover, SQL Server 2012 allows you to perform various administrative tasks like backup of data, in case original data is lost or deleted for any reason, recovery of that data and provide capabilities for disaster recovery (DR).

Prior to its current avatar, we had earlier versions of SQL Server 6.0/2000/2005/2008/2008R2, first version SQL Server 1.0 came out way back in 1989, but, the latest edition of SQL Server 2012 has got the core database engine more robust, richer in features and provides tighter integration with Business Intelligence Development (BID) along with various debugging capabilities. Besides multitude of database management (DBMS) features, SQL Server comes with a stack of tools to enrich the database lifecycle (DBLC) experience: SQL Server Integration Services (SSIS) for manipulation of data, SQL Server Reporting Services (SSRS) for reports and SQL Server Analysis Services (SSAS) for designing OLAP (Online Analytical Processing) cubes, data warehousing and data mining.

Other than Microsoft (MS) SQL Server 2012, there are several other prominent RDBMSs like Oracle, MySQL, DB2, Informix, Sybase, PostgreSQL, and Teradata. In past, MS-Access and FoxPro were also used for storing data. All RDBMSs are based on the relational model as propounded by Dr. E. F. Codd and a set of so-called 12 rules that Dr. Codd defined to qualify a pure RDBMS. Since its debut, SQL Server is increasingly becoming popular, especially after Microsoft released a fully functionality free SQL Server Express Editions. Therefore, learning and having knowledge of SQL Server is very beneficial.

### *Why this book:*

The approach has been to explain SQL Server in plain English and get the readers started with SQL Server 2012 on their own machine and learn it. Even if you are a beginner, you can get going on SQL Server 2012 by following this book. This book will walk you systemically about SQL Server 2012 Express Edition installation procedure, SQL queries, Stored Procedures, Functions, Views, Triggers, Indexes, with step by step guidance.

Note that this book is not about programming and if you were looking to learn programming, this book is not for you. But, if you want to get started quickly with SQL Server 2012, this book is for you. It is by no-means meant to be a comprehensive book, but, this is a beginner's guide to SQL Server 2012 to get you started quickly and hit the ground running. You can get the best value out of this book by opening this book on one monitor while doing all the steps on another monitor, not by skimming thru this book. Once you have followed and performed all the steps in this book, you can refer to other reference books and blog articles.

Happy SQL'ing!

## Chapter 2: SQL Server 2012 Installation Procedure

1. Before starting the SQL Server 2012 Express installation procedure, check the following items:
   a. Processor Type: x64 (64 bits) or x86 (32 bits). Press **Start**-> Right click (not Click) on **Computer** -> Click **Properties,** as in below Figure. You will be downloading SQL Server 2012 according to the processor type and it is important to confirm it before proceeding any further.

   View basic information about your computer

   Windows edition

      Windows 7 Home Premium

      Copyright © 2009 Microsoft Corporation.  All rights reserved.

      Service Pack 1
      Get more features with a new edition of Windows 7

   System

   | | |
   |---|---|
   | Manufacturer: | Lenovo |
   | Model: | Lenovo Win7 PC |
   | Rating: | **4.7** Windows Experience Index |
   | Processor: | Intel(R) Core(TM) i5-2430M CPU @ 2.40GHz   2.40 GHz |
   | Installed memory (RAM): | 8.00 GB |
   | System type: | 64-bit Operating System |
   | Pen and Touch: | No Pen or Touch Input is available for this Display |

   b. Memory: At-least 1 GB recommended, though, minimum is 512MB.
   c. Hard disk: At-least 6GB of available disk space on the system drive.
   d. Create a new folder **C:\Downloads** using *Windows Explorer* as a place holder to keep all the downloaded software.
   e. Download and install .Net Framework 3.5 Service Pack 1 from following URL:
      http://www.microsoft.com/en-us/download/details.aspx?id=22
   f. Download and install .Net Framework 4.0 from following URL:
      http://www.microsoft.com/en-us/download/details.aspx?id=3324

2. Download the installation files from the following URL and save it on your machine
   http://www.microsoft.com/en-us/download/details.aspx?id=29062

   ☑  ENU\x64\SQLEXPRWT_x64_ENU.exe          669.9 MB

In case you have MSDN subscription, you can download by logging into your account and downloading from there.

SQL Server 2012 Express Edition (for 64 bits operating system) comes in following flavors:

i. LocalDB MSI (**SqlLocalDB.MSI**): It is a lightweight edition to work with code.

ii. SQL Server Express (**SQLEXPR_x64_ENU.exe**): It contains only core database engine.

iii. SQL Server Management Studio (**SQLManagementStudio_x64_ENU.exe**): It contains only the management tools without the database server engine.

iv. SQL Server Express with Tools (**SQLEXPRWT_x64_ENU.exe**): It contains all the management tools along with configuration as database server engine. *We will use this particular edition in this book.*

v. SQL Server Express with Advanced Tools (**SQLEXPRADV_x64_ENU.exe**): It contains all the wells and whistle that comes along with SQL Server 2012, like reporting services and full text search capabilities.

Run the installation by double clicking on the **SQLEXPRWT_x64_ENU.exe** file that you downloaded earlier on your local machine in folder *C:\Downloads* or the folder where you saved it while downloading it.

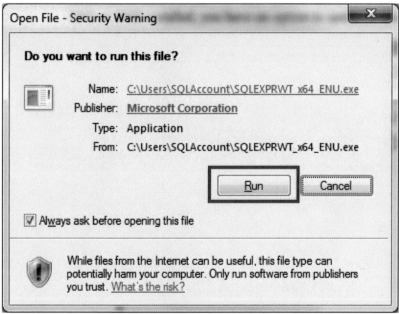

NOTE: *In case you have x86 processor on your Windows operating system, you will need to use corresponding version of above mentioned flavors.*

3. Click **Run**. Files are extracted and copied to the directory as mentioned in message box.

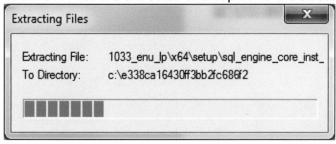

A security **User Account Control** message box is displayed: "Do you want to allow the following program to make changes to this computer?" to get your confirmation for changing changes to your machine by SQL Server 2012. Click **Yes** to proceed further.

Note: *This message box may be minimized at the bottom, so, look for a flashing icon at the bottom of the screen.*

4. Select **New SQL Server stand-alone installation** in right side panel as below:

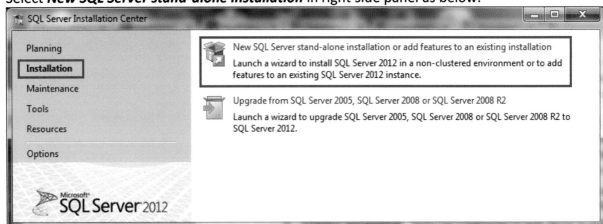

Installation will check for product updates and start install setup as below.

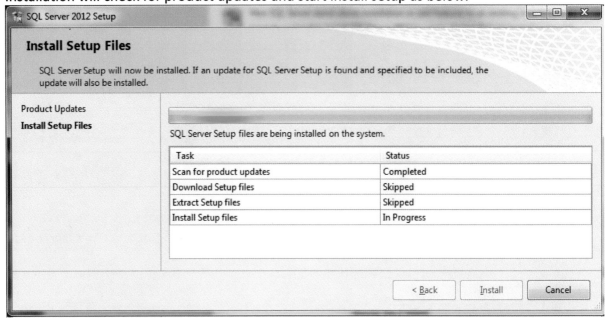

4. In **License Terms** screen, checkmark **I Accept the license terms**, if you agree with terms and Click **Next**.

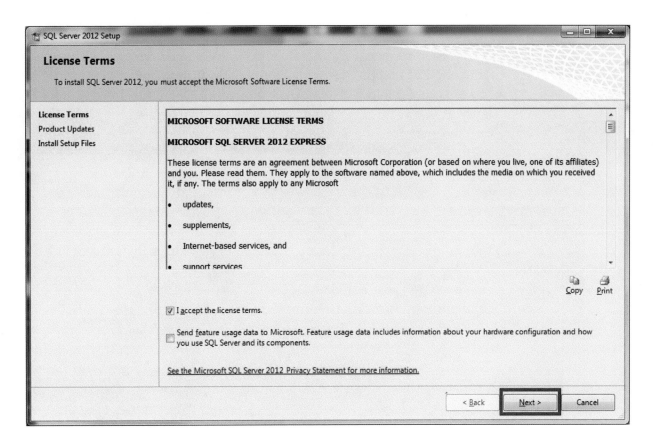

5.  In **Product Updates** screen, click **Next**, in case there are updates found by the installation setup, they will be displayed and will be installed.

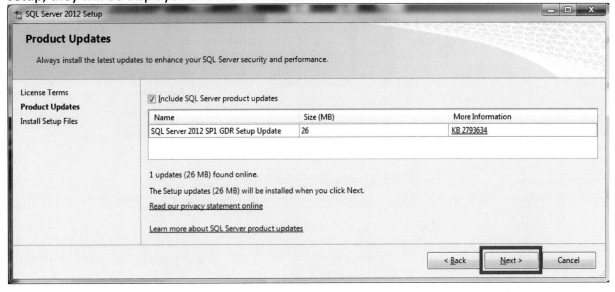

You will be displayed a **Setup Support Rules screen,** as below, showing the status of various tests made by Installation to check whether the machine satisfies all the required pre-requisites. If there is any failure, it would need to be resolved before proceeding. Firewall warning message can be ignored for now and installation can still continue.

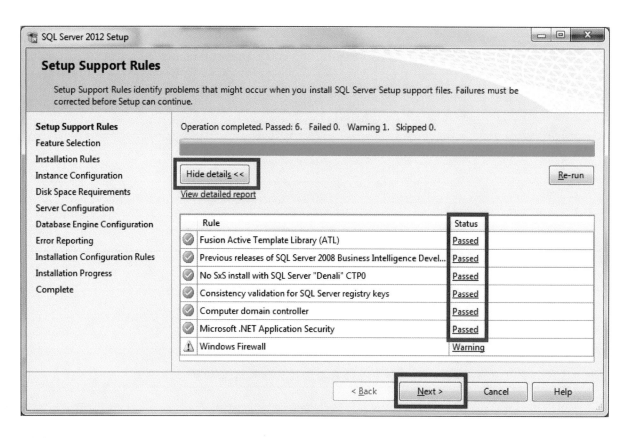

6. Click **Next** in **Setup Support Rules** and you will be asked to select the features that you want to install, we will select all features **Select All**. Note the prerequisites mentioned.

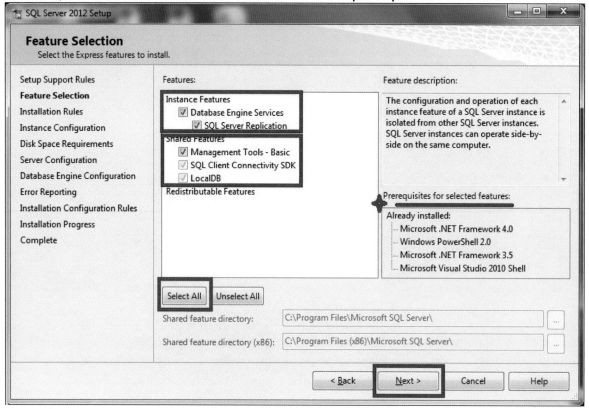

7. **Instance Configuration** screen will prompt you to assign an instance name, as in below Fig. Enter **SQLEXPRESS2012** as Named Instance.

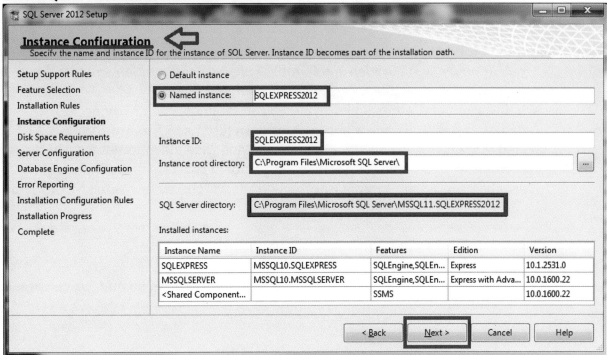

Note: It is important to understand the concept of an **SQL Instance**. It is a unit or a container that consists of one or more databases, services, and other configuration settings and is assigned a Name or ID for its unique identification on a machine. You can install more than one SQL *Instances* that work side by side on the same machine.

8. Click **Next** in **Instance Configuration** screen and you will be displayed **Server Configuration** screen where you can set the startup type and accounts used by SQL Server Database Engine and SQL Server Browser, we will keep default accounts.

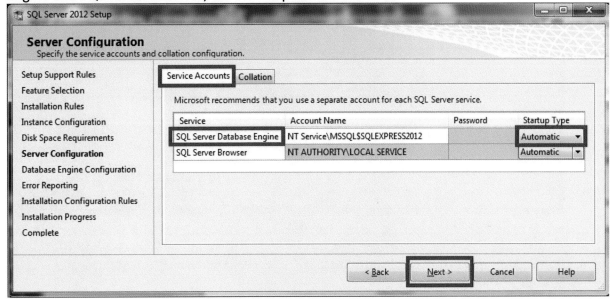

We will keep the **Collation** as SQL_Latin1_General_CP1_CI_AS: Latin1-General, **C**ase-**I**nsensitive, **A**ccent-**S**ensitive for Unicode data. This instructs to SQL Server how it stores data. Collation can be customized and changed for a different language. We will use the default setting.

9. Click **Next** in **Server Configuration** and **Database Engine Configuration** screen is displayed, as in below Fig. Note that there are 2 *Authentication Mode*:
   a. **Windows Authentication mode**: If you select this option, you can connect to SQL Server Database Engine *only* using windows credentials (username/password).
   b. **Mixed Mode** (SQL Server authentication and Windows Authentication): If you choose this option, you can connect to SQL Server Database Engine with *both* windows credentials and system account (sa) account. We will choose this Mixed Mode option.

   *It is strongly recommended that you note down the password that you are entering and keep it handy for future use. We will use it in Chapter 3.*

   **Note:** You will add SQL Server Administrator or admins by clicking on **Add Current User** (if current account does not already exist). These accounts will have unrestricted access to the Database engine.

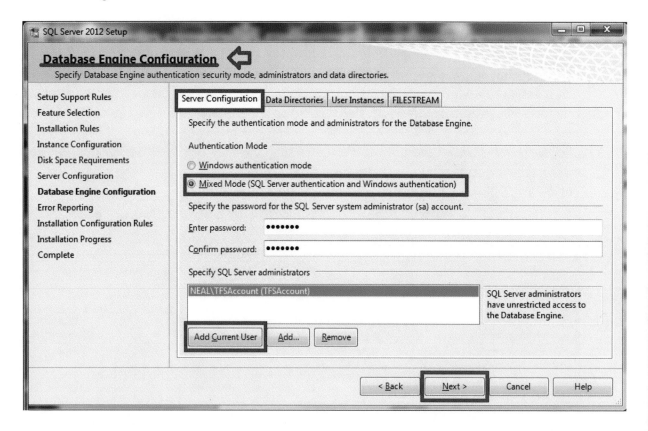

Check the **Data Directories** as below and we will keep the default settings (unless you want to use some other drive than C:\ drive to install SQL Server) and also User Instances and FileStream settings.

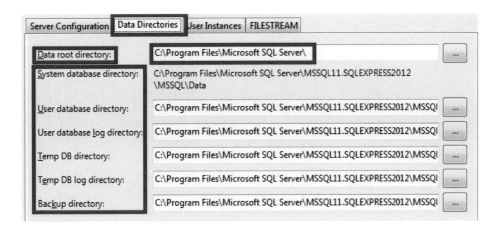

10. Click **Next** in **Database Engine Configuration** screen. **Error Reporting** is displayed, as in below Fig.

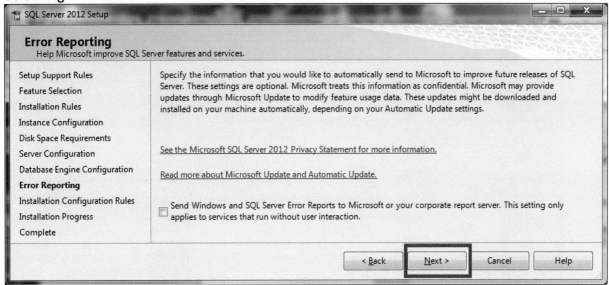

In case you want to send error reports to Microsoft/Corporate report server, you may check mark this option in above screen.

Note: *In case you want to change any option, you can press **Back** and make changes accordingly now.* This is the last **Next** to press. Installation will start copying the required files to your local machine and no more changes can be made.

11. Click **Next** in **Error Reporting** and Installation will displayed an **Installation Progress** screen, as below.

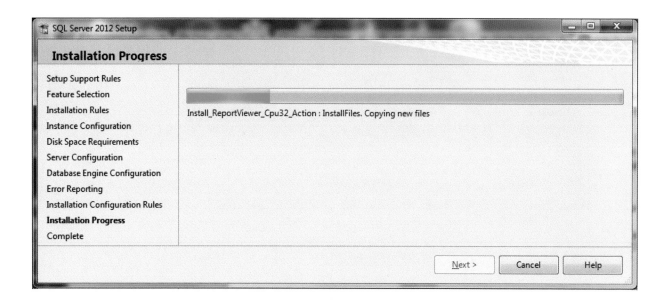

12. Finally, **Complete** screen is displayed as in below Fig.

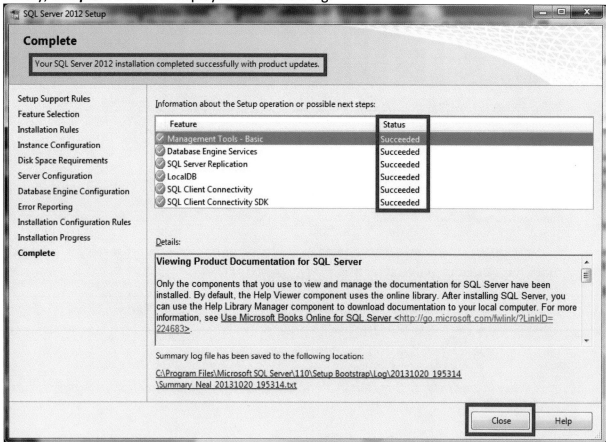

13. Press **Close** to close the screen and installation is successfully completed.

14. Go to *Start* -> Click *All Programs* and you will notice that SQL Server 2012 is added to the menu as in below Fig.

If you reached to this step, you are ready to use your favorite SQL Server Management Studio (SSMS) and explore how to run SQL queries, create database diagrams, and other good stuff.

In next Chapter 3, we will see how we can connect to the SQL Server Instance that was installed in above steps and start using SQL Server Management Studio (SSMS).

## Chapter 3: SQL Server 2012 Management Studio (SSMS)

This chapter and rest of the chapters will systematically walk you thru various features of SQL Server Management Studio like Server Explorer, Solution Explorer, Object Explorer, T-SQL Query Editor, Activity Monitor, Template Explorer, Tools, Log file Viewer, Options, Execution Plan, SQL Profiler, Query Designer, etc. and connect to SQL Server Instance and learn to work with a database.

### 3.1 OVERVIEW SSMS

Open SQL Server Management Studio 2012: **Start -> All Programs -> SQL Server Management Studio** (an icon image that looks like a cylinder with a hammer, as below).

**Connect to Server** screen is displayed as below in Fig.

It is possible that Server name may already be populated, e.g., **NEAL\SQLEXPRESS2012** (**Machine name\SQL Server Instance name).** Instance name is the one that we entered in **Chapter 2, Step 7.** Machine name can be found using **Chapter 2, Step 1a:** Press *Start*-> Right click (not Click) on *Computer* -> Click *Properties*

In case Server Name is empty**,** Press triangular arrow down selection button in **Server Name** and Click *<Browse for more...>* option**,** as in below Fig.

Another dialog box will be displayed as in below Fig. Under **Local Servers**, Click on **"+"** node and you will see the SQL Server Instance that was installed earlier in Chapter 2, as in below Fig. Select **NEAL\SQLSERVER2012** option listed there**.**

Now, Server name should be populated that you can connect to and work with. But, we need to choose authentication method as explained in next step.

## 3.2 CREATE CONNECTION TO SQL Server

There are 2 ways to authenticating while connecting to SQL Server:

a. **_Windows Authentication_**:  If you are seeing above Figs., you are already logged to your local machine & authenticated by windows and hence, SQL Server allows you to connect to SQL server by using same windows credentials (username and password). Click **_Connect_** to create a connection to SQL Server instance that was installed in Chapter 2.

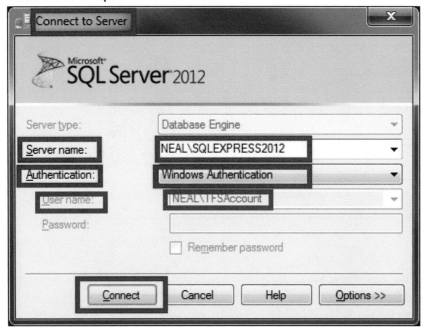

You will be taken to SQL Server Management Studio (SSMS) or just **Studio** in brief and **Object Explorer** panel will be displayed as in below Fig. Note that both **SQL Server Instance** name: **NEAL\SQLEXPRESS2012** and Windows account used: **NEAL\TFSAccount** is displayed.

Note that your access to different SQL Server objects will depend upon the roles and permissions assigned to your windows account, normally by a DBA (Database Admin) inside an organization. However, as you added your local windows account in **Chapter 2, Step 9** to list of System Administrator accounts, therefore, you have full privilege to perform any operation on SQL Server Instance that was created in Chapter 2.

OR use SQL Server authentication as in Step 2b below.

b. **SQL Server Authentication**: In Chapter 2, Step 9, we created a **System Administrator (sa)** account and entered password. We will use that account to connect to SQL Server. Enter **Login:** *sa* and **Password:** *password* (use the password that you noted down earlier in Chapter 2)

Now, you will be taken to SQL Server Management Studio and **Object Explorer** panel will be displayed.

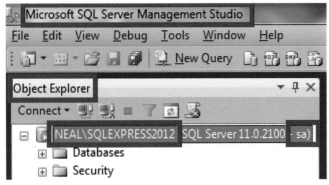

Note that as System Administrator, you will have complete control over the SQL Server Instance and all the objects inside that instance, including assigning roles to other Windows OR SQL Accounts.

*Note that you can use either Windows or SQL Server authentication, but, most of the demos in this book will be using Windows Authentication.*

## 3.3 OBJECT EXPLORER

**Object Explorer:** Object Explorer is one of the most important tools in SQL Server Management Studio (SSMS) as, most of the SQL objects will be managed via Object Explorer. Click on "+" icon image near green arrow mark and you will be displayed expanded view under SQL Server Instance connection as in below Fig, (a partial view is shown to conserve space). Following SQL objects are displayed:

a. **Databases**: This SQL object contains **System Databases** and user created **Databases**. Further, a database can itself contain various tables, indexes, constraints, functions, stored procedures, triggers, etc. as we will see in detail in later chapters.

b. **Security**: It contains login accounts, roles and credentials objects.

c. **Server Objects**: It has objects that are defined at Server level like Linked Servers to connect to other SQL Servers deployed on different machines.

d. **Replication**: This object is used for a copy of database at some remote location for disaster recovery purposes or even for reporting server, so that pulling reports does not put a stress on the regular OLTP transactional database SQL Server.

e. **Management**: It houses other management related objects like policy management, extended events for system health and server logs. Note that Enterprise edition or Advanced Tools SQL Server editions come with some additional features like full-text search and online indexing.

Note that if you ever loose **Object Explorer** window or if it gets hidden, you can always get it back by Click -> **View** menu item on Management Studio's toolbar at the top.

Object Explorer has a small little triangle caret icon that can be used to position this window and has following options:

a. *Float*: floats object explorer window anywhere inside Management Studio (SSMS) or even outside SSMS, which is known as ***tear-out*** feature. If you have multiple monitors, this feature is very helpful in placing object explorer on a $2^{nd}$ or $3^{rd}$ monitor while SSMS is on $1^{st}$ monitor. Tear-out is a new feature of SQL Server 2012.

b. *Dock:* The window is docked or placed to the left, right, top or bottom edge of the Management Studio window.

c. *Hide:* Use of this option causes the object explorer window to be hidden or removed from the Management Studio and you would need to go to **View -> Object Explorer** to bring it back.

Besides triangle caret for window position, there is an additional icon: *pin*, shown with vertical direction in above Fig. If you click on this pin, Object Explorer window will be minimized to the edge, or in order words, it will be *unpinned* from Studio' window, as shown in below Fig.

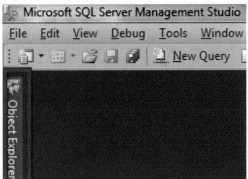

When mouse arrow is hovered over above *unpinned* Object Explorer (in above Fig), it will pop out as in below Fig. Note that pin icon is placed horizontally, indicating its *unpinned* status.

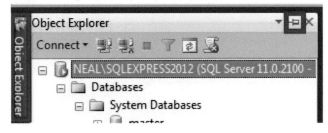

If you click on *unpinned* icon, Object Explorer will be pinned to the Studio's window permanently, unless it is unpinned or closed.

## 3.4 QUERY EDITOR

**Query Editor**: This is another important window where you will be running most T-SQL queries (e.g., SELECT). There are following 3 ways to open this query editor:

a. Click **New Query** button the Studio's toolbar, as shown in below Fig. A new blank window will appear with title **SQLQuery1** along with account used. OR

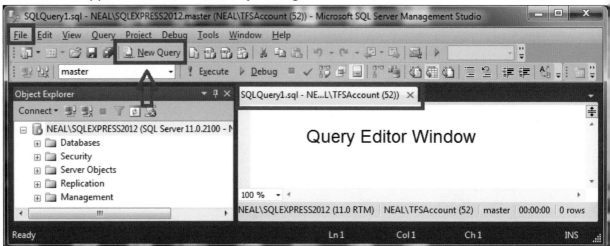

b. Click **File -> New -> Query with Current Connection** and you will see Query Editor Window displayed as above. OR

c. Press **CTL + N** keys together. A new Query Editor Window is displayed as in above Fig. This combination of keys is also known as *hot keys*.

**Options**: Click **Tools -> Options**. An Options window is displayed as below. It is used for settings various options as enumerated below.

a. **Environment:** Fonts and colors, documents, keyboard and general settings.

b. **Source Control**: Plug-in for source control can be changed.

c. **Text Editor**: File Extension, Text, T-SQL, Intellisense feature, etc. can be set. Intellisense allows you to type in few initial letters and SQL Server editor (above fig) will try to find best match for those letters and auto-populate complete words for you and thereby helping in saving some typing.

d. **Query Execution:** Execution time-out, row counts can be changed.

e. **Query Results**: Save result to document, grid, display result in a separate tab

f. **Designers**: Transaction time-out, various warnings can be set.

g. SQL Server **AlwaysOn**: These are settings for High availability: refresh interval, etc.

h. **SQL Server Object Explorer**: You can set how many rows to return when you run SQL select statement. By default, 1000 rows are returned and 200 rows for edit mode. But, if you do not want to see 1000 rows, and just 10 or 100 first rows, change this setting and it helps in quick viewing of sample data, especially if you just need to see only few rows.

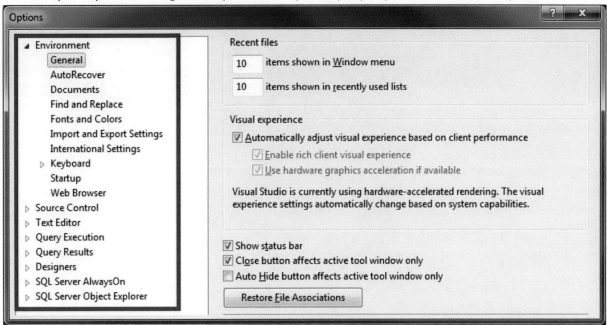

NOTE: *It is recommended that you change following setting*: Remove check mark in **"Prevent saving changes that require table re-creation"** under **Designers** section, otherwise you will not be able to save changes in tables made thru table designer. It is better to change this default setting right now.

In next Chapter 4, we will see how to create a new database, tables, constraints, and run the T-SQL queries.

## *Chapter 4: Create Database, Table Schema, Fields, PK, Constraints*

After getting familiar with Studio and various features of Studio, this chapter will lay a foundation to the creation of database, tables within a database, fields or columns and rows or records consisting of fields/columns within a table, various constraints, primary and foreign keys and other SQL objects. All these SQL objects constitute a **physical database**. Normally, you will be designing a **logical database** first to satisfy customer/stakeholders requirements and then design the actual physical database. But, we will start working on physical database first as a starting point in this chapter.

We will begin with a simple database model where the requirements are to create customers who can place orders for products. So, we will house this information into 3 tables: Customers, Orders and Products. These 3 tables will be placed inside a new database: **IMS**, short for Inventory Management System.

### 4.1 CREATE DATABASE

1. Open Studio: *Start -> All Programs -> Microsoft SQL Server 2012 -> SQL Server Management Studio.*
2. Connect to SQL Server Instance**:** Studio should already be populated with Server name and authentication info and if yes, Press *Connect.* If not, follow steps as elaborated in previous Chapter 3.
3. Right Click on *Databases* node, as shown in below figure and choose *New Database...* option.

**New Database** screen will be displayed as in below Fig.
4. Enter *IMS* in Database name and leave owner as *<default>* for now.

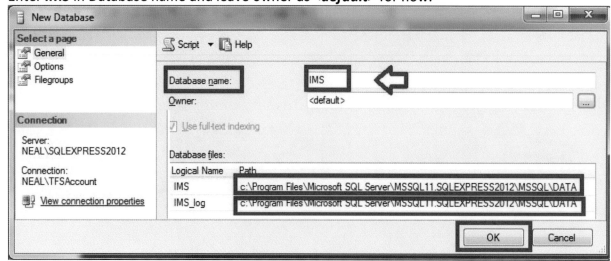

The database file names are automatically assigned based on the database name that you entered. Note the paths of 2 database files:

a. **.mdf** file: IMS.mdf is the primary *m*ain *d*atabase *f*ile that stores actual data and located: **C:\Program Files\Microsoft SQL Server\MSSQL11.SQLEXPRESS2012\MSSQL\Data\**

b. **.ldf** file: IMS_log.ldf is the transaction *l*og *d*atabase *f*ile that saves the logging details of actual data when it is inserted, deleted or updated. This file is located in same above folder. However, it is considered a good practice to place mdf and ldf files in separate drive.

Note that there can be a secondary database file (**.ndf**) that can be used to store some tables in a separate drive to improve performance.

5. Press **OK**. SQL Server will create a database with following default values:

a. Initial Size: 3MB with auto growth of 1 MB, means that when database file is filled up to 3MB, it will automatically increase the size of IMS.mdf file by 1 MB every time and maximum size being the available drive space on your local machine.

b. Log file: IMS_log.ldf file is initially assigned with 1MB of space and it will grow automatically by 10% every time when 1MB is filled up.

You can change these files using the ellipses and also these file names. But, we will leave the default names and sizes assigned by SQL Server.

You will see an entry **IMS** created under databases node, as shown in below Fig. This is the new database that we just created.

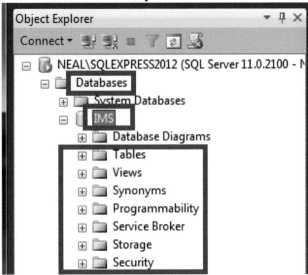

## 4.2 SYSTEM DATABASES

Note that there is also **System Databases** entry that is created by default by SQL Server. System Databases consist of following 4 databases:

a. **master**
b. **model**
c. **msdb**

d. *tempdb*

In case you want to see the T-SQL query that can be used to create the new database, Right Click (not click) on **IMS** under Databases node **-> *Script Database as* -> *Create to* -> *New Query Editor Window.*** You will see following *Create Database* T-SQL query:

```
CREATE DATABASE [IMS]
   CONTAINMENT = NONE
   ON PRIMARY
   (NAME = N'IMS', FILENAME = N'c:\Program Files\Microsoft SQL
   Server\MSSQL11.SQLEXPRESS2012\MSSQL\DATA\IMS.mdf', SIZE = 3072KB,
   MAXSIZE = UNLIMITED, FILEGROWTH = 1024KB )
   LOG ON
   (NAME = N'IMS_log', FILENAME = N'c:\Program Files\Microsoft SQL
   Server\MSSQL11.SQLEXPRESS2012\MSSQL\DATA\IMS_log.ldf', SIZE = 1024KB,
   MAXSIZE = 2048GB , FILEGROWTH = 10%)
GO
```

You could have very well used above T-SQL in Query Editor Window and it would also have created same new database that we created earlier. But, our good old friend by now: *Studio* saves some typing for us and makes our life easier.

Now, we have created a new database and it is now turn to create tables inside that database. Tables are data structures that contain the actual data as we will see.

## 4.3 CREATE TABLE

1. **Create Table**: Right Click *Tables* under IMS node-> *New Table...* A new window: Table Designer will be displayed, with headings: Column Name, Data Type and whether to allow Null value for that column, as in below Fig. Data Type represents the type of data that will be stored in that column/field, e.g. an integer, decimal or characters, as we will see later.

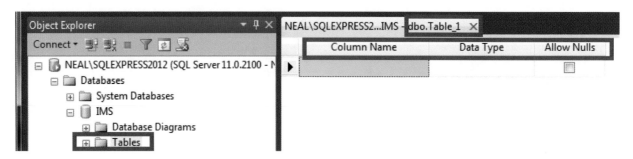

Following are some of the *common* data types that SQL Server uses for each column/field.
a. *Int*: Allows whole number, e.g. 1, 50000, etc. within limits: max. Or min. value.
b. *Decimal*: Allows decimal values with customizable significant and decimal places.
c. *Varchar:* Allows a *var*iable length *char*acters and contain alpha-numeric (letters and numbers) and special characters.

d. **DateTime:** Allows a date and time data, e.g., 2010-01-01 00:00:00 (YYYY-MM-DD HH:MM:SS)

*Null* value is a special value that represents whether the data that we will store in that column/field can be empty or not-empty; many times column/field is referred as **Null**able or **Not-Null**able column. Note that **Null** value strictly is not same as blank or even a space value, rather it is a special value stored inside SQL Server that represents emptiness for that particular column. Putting a check mark in **Allow Nulls** tag indicates that Null values are allowed to be stored for that column and absence of check mark indicates that Null values will not be allowed to be entered, you would need to enter some value depending upon the declared data type. If you try to enter value of any other data type (e.g. enter a decimal value while column is declared as integer type), SQL Server will give you an error message, or in technical terms: *a SQL Exception is thrown by SQL Server that can be captured for error handling*, as we will later in details.

Next, we will look at IMS database design and model. Also, **normalization** process needs to be considered while designing database schema, we will continue with modeling of database schema first so that you can get a feel of the actual database and how it is created and maintained in Studio.

2. Enter following columns for the new customer table: **TblCustomer** with appropriate type of data that each column is going to store.
a. *CustomerID*: Int, Not-Null, Primary Key
b. *FirstName*: Varchar(50): (max. 50 character size), Not-Null (means value is required)
c. *MiddleName*: Varchar(10)
d. *LastName*: Varchar(50), Not-Null
e. *Address*: Varchar(100), Not-Null
f. *City*: Varchar(50), Not-Null
g. *State*: Varchar(25), Not-Null
h. *ZipCode*: Varchar(10), Not-Null
i. *Phone*: Varchar(15)
j. *Country*: Varchar(25)

3. Choose **int** from drop down list under **Data Type** and remove check mark for *CustomerID* column under **Allow Nulls** and, as in below Fig.

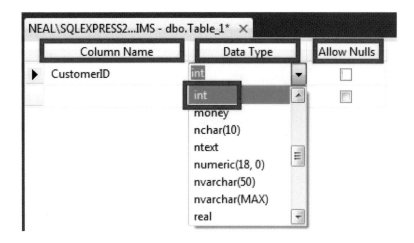

## 4.4 CREATE PRIMARY KEY (PK)

1. CustomerID is Customer identification number and we want this column to store only unique/distinct and *Not-Null* values: this means that none of the value stored in this column can be same and also none of the values can be *Null*. This ensures uniqueness of each CustomerID value entered and helps in faster retrieval of data also, as we will see in Chapter on Indexes.

Click on *Lock* ( ) icon in toolbar to set CustomerID as Primary key, as shown in below Fig.

Note that when you create a Primary Key (PK), a *clustered index* is automatically created by SQL Server and explained in details in Chapter 7.

2. Enter rest of the columns as defined in Step 7 with appropriate data types and size. Note: It is important to type-in both type and size of each column; otherwise, SQL Server will display error message if the entered value does not conform to these column definitions.

Once you have entered all the columns, **TblCustomer** table will look as in below Fig. in *table designer* window.

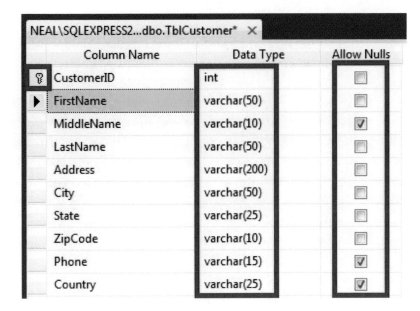

3. Click on **Save** icon on toolbar OR Click on **File -> Save Table_1** and **Choose Name** message box will be displayed as in below Fig. Enter name of the table: **TblCustomer** and press **OK**.

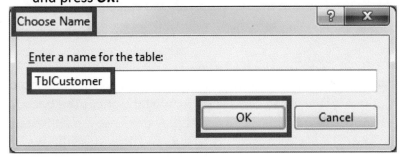

4. **Create Table Using T-SQL**: Right Click on **TblCustomer** node **-> Script Table as -> Create to -> New Query Editor Window**. A new query editor window displays the SQL query that can create the same table that we created in previous Steps.

```
CREATE TABLE [dbo].[TblCustomer](
    [CustomerID] [int] NOT NULL,
    [FirstName] [varchar](50) NOT NULL,
    [MiddleName] [varchar](10) NULL,
    [LastName] [varchar](50) NOT NULL,
    [Address] [varchar](200) NOT NULL,
    [City] [varchar](50) NOT NULL,
    [State] [varchar](25) NOT NULL,
    [ZipCode] [varchar](10) NOT NULL,
    [Phone] [varchar](15) NULL,
    [Country] [varchar](25) NULL,
 CONSTRAINT [PK_TblCustomer] PRIMARY KEY CLUSTERED ([CustomerID] ASC )
WITH (PAD_INDEX = OFF, STATISTICS_NORECOMPUTE = OFF, IGNORE_DUP_KEY = OFF,
ALLOW_ROW_LOCKS = ON, ALLOW_PAGE_LOCKS = ON) ON [PRIMARY]
) ON [PRIMARY]
```

You will notice that **TblCustomer** table is now displayed under *Tables* under IMS database in Object Explorer. If it is not immediately displayed, Right Click on *Tables* node -> *Refresh* and Customer table will be displayed.

Note that in case you made some mistake or need to make changes in table for any other reason, you can always open the table in design view by: Right Click on **TblCustomer** table -> **Design**. Now, you can revise the table schema and save it again. Similarly, if you want to remove Primary Key from a column, select that column and Click on *Lock* ( 🔒 ) icon and do not forget to press **Save**, especially, *it is easy to miss pressing Save* button in the excitement of making changes and later on not seeing those changes in table after refresh. It is not a Studio problem; it's just that you did not press Save once you are done with your changes.

**Naming Convention**: There is a wide variety of opinion regarding naming of various SQL objects. We named customer table as **TblCustomer** where 3 initial letters: **Tbl** represents a table. Reason we choose to follow this naming convention for a table is due to the fact that it is easy to recognize any table in the whole database if it is prefixed with these 3 letters which helps in identifying all the tables, without anyone else having to explain where and what all tables are. If you knew that tables are named with **Tbl**, you will come to associate these 3 initials with a table. Similarly, we will prefix other SQL objects for easy identification.

It is considered a good practice to consistently follow a standard naming convention within a department or even an organization. Every company will typically have their own standard naming conventions and sometimes you will see Gurus debating which one is the best one. It is not important what conventions are followed, *as long as they are followed consistently across the board and by all.* Generally, a development (dev) lead or DBA or Architect or some sr. team member will define these naming conventions for the whole team/ department to follow. *It is strongly recommended to have a standard naming convention in place for good coding practices.*

## 4.5 IDENTITY

1. **CustomerID Identity**: Many times, we want to let SQL Server assign an integer/whole number *automatically* without providing explicitly a number in SQL Insert query statement. This helps in management of Customer ID without us keeping track of what the next Customer ID needs to be assigned to a new customer. We will let SQL Server assign a Customer ID to a new customer.

2. Take your mouse cursor to *CustomerID* in table designer and highlight this column, as shown in below Fig. Right Click on **TblCustomer** node under *Tables* in Object Explorer -> In **Column Properties** window, Click on **Identity Specification** property listed -> Double Click on **(Is Identity)** OR choose **Yes** from drop down list. **Identity Increment** is populated to 1: meaning that a new value of CustomerID will increase by 1 every time a new record is

added and **Identity Seed** is assigned as 1, indicating that initial value will start/seed with 1. Both Identity Increment and Identity Seed can be changed.

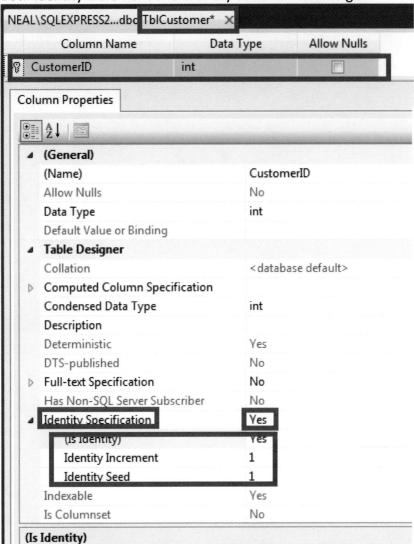

Press **Save** to save the changes in table schema of **TblCustomer** table.

3. Right Click **Tables -> New Tables...** and enter the columns for product table: **TblProduct** as enumerated below:
   a. **ProductID**, *Int, Not-Null, Primary Key*
   b. **Name**, *Varchar(50), Not-Null*
   c. **Description**, *Varchar(100)*
   d. **Manufacturer**, *Varchar(50)*
   e. **QtyAvailable**, *Int, Not-Null*
   f. **Price**, *Decimal(9,2)*: this allows you to enter 7 (=9-2) significant digits number and up to 2 decimal places, e.g., 1234567.99, i.e., a product with a max price of $10 Million, less 1 cent, which should cover price range of most of the common products, even a product like personal yacht, except for a higher end.

4. Click on **Lock** icon on *ProductID* to set it as a *Primary Key* and you will see a lock icon attached with ProductID column. Once columns are added using the table designer window, it will look as in below Fig.

| Column Name | Data Type | Allow Nulls |
|---|---|---|
| ProductID | int | ☐ |
| Name | varchar(50) | ☐ |
| Description | varchar(100) | ☑ |
| Manufacturer | varchar(50) | ☑ |
| QtyAvailable | int | ☐ |
| Price | decimal(9, 2) | ☑ |

NEAL\SQLEXPRESS20...- dbo.TblProduct ✕

5. Press **Save** to save the columns and type-in the name of this new table as **TblProduct**. In order to view this newly added table, Right Click on *Tables* node in Object Explorer and Choose *Refresh*, you will see **TblProduct** table listed. Now, in order to view the T-SQL required to generate this table, Right Click on *TblProduct* node *-> Script Table as -> Create to -> New Query Editor Window*. A new query editor window displays the SQL query that can create the same table that we created in this Step.

```
CREATE TABLE [dbo].[TblProduct](
    [ProductID] [int] IDENTITY(1,1) NOT NULL,
    [Name] [varchar](50) NOT NULL,
    [Description] [varchar](100) NULL,
    [Manufacturer] [varchar](50) NULL,
    [QtyAvailable] [int] NOT NULL,
    [Price] [decimal](9, 2) NULL,
    CONSTRAINT [PK_TblProduct] PRIMARY KEY CLUSTERED ([ProductID] ASC)
    WITH (PAD_INDEX = OFF,STATISTICS_NORECOMPUTE = OFF,IGNORE_DUP_KEY =
    OFF, ALLOW_ROW_LOCKS = ON, ALLOW_PAGE_LOCKS = ON) ON [PRIMARY]) ON
    [PRIMARY]
```

Customers are going to order products and that order information is stored in **TblOrder** table as we will see in next step.

5. Right Click *Tables -> New Tables...* and enter the columns for order table: *TblOrder* as below:
a. **OrderID**, *Int, Not Null, Primary Key*
b. **CustomerID**: *Int, Not Null, Foreign key*: we will see how to create this in next few steps.
c. **ProductID**: *Int, Not Null, Foreign Key*
d. **OrderQty**: *Int, Not Null*
e. **OrderDate:** *DateTime, Not Null*
f. **IsOrderActive**: *Bit, Not Null*
g. **Comment**: *Varchar(100)*

6.  Click on **Lock** icon on OrderID to set it as a *Primary Key* and you will see a lock icon attached with OrderID column. After addition of above columns, the table will look as in below Fig.

| Column Name | Data Type | Allow Nulls |
|---|---|---|
| OrderID | int | ☐ |
| CustomerID | int | ☐ |
| ProductID | int | ☐ |
| OrderQty | int | ☐ |
| OrderDate | datetime | ☐ |
| IsOrderActive | bit | ☐ |
| Comment | varchar(100) | ☑ |

NEAL\SQLEXPRESS2...MS - dbo.TblOrder ✕

7.  Press **Save** to save the columns and type-in the name of this new table as **TbOrder**. In order to view this newly added table, Right Click on *Tables* node in Object Explorer and Choose *Refresh*, you will see **TblOrder** table listed. Now, in order to view the T-SQL required to generate this table, Right Click on *TblOrder* node *-> Script Table as -> Create to -> New Query Editor Window*. A new query editor window displays the SQL query that can create the same table that we created in this Step.

```
CREATE TABLE [dbo].[TblOrder](
    [OrderID] [int] NOT NULL,
    [CustomerID] [int] NOT NULL,
    [ProductID] [int] NOT NULL,
    [OrderQty] [int] NOT NULL,
    [OrderDate] [datetime] NOT NULL,
    [IsOrderActive] [bit] NOT NULL,
    [Comment] [varchar](100) NULL,
    CONSTRAINT [PK_TblOrder] PRIMARY KEY CLUSTERED ([OrderID] ASC ) WITH
    (PAD_INDEX = OFF, STATISTICS_NORECOMPUTE = OFF, IGNORE_DUP_KEY = OFF,
    ALLOW_ROW_LOCKS = ON, ALLOW_PAGE_LOCKS = ON) ON [PRIMARY]) ON [PRIMARY]
```

All 3 tables: **TblCustomer, TblProduct and TblOrder** are listed in below Fig. and **TblCustomer** table is shown in expanded node view. This is how your view should look like.

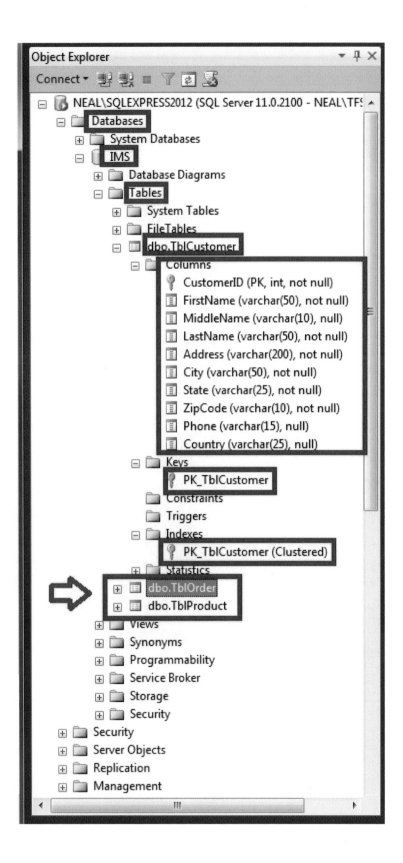

# 4.5 CONSTRAINTS

**Constraints**: So far in this chapter, we have seen various rules specified for the column values that it can store and these rules are technically called as **SQL Constraints** or simply **Constraints**, e.g., NOT NULL, where value entered in a column like CustomerID cannot be **Null**. SQL Server contains following *constraints*:

a. **NOT NULL Constraint**: Values stored in a column cannot be a NULL value.

b. **UNIQUE Constraint**: Column values stored in each row/record, must be a unique/distinct value

c. **PRIMARY KEY Constraint**: Combination of above **NOT NULL** and **UNIQUE** *constraints*. We created PK in earlier steps for 3 tables.

d. **FOREIGN KEY Constraint:** This constraint helps in maintaining the integrity of data that in stored in different tables and is explained in next step.

e. **CHECK Constraint**: This constraint helps in applying a specific condition to the values stored in a column, e.g., values stored are greater than 0.

f. **DEFAULT Constraint**: It is used to set a default (fixed) value when no value is specified in Insert T-SQL query, e.g., if we want to store current system date and time, we can specify a default system date & time to store in a column and there would be no need to explicitly mention a date time and SQL Server will automatically assign a value. In other cases, you may want to specify a static value of 0 so that column value is seeded with an initial value to begin with so that it does not remain empty. This is very useful in auto-populating a column with an initial value without being provided in the query.


# 4.5 FOREIGN KEYS (FK)

**Foreign Keys**:

A foreign key (FK) in a table (*foreign-keyed table* or *child table*) is a column that is really a *primary key* in another table (*primary-keyed table* or *parent* table). For e.g., *CustomerID* is primary key in *TblCustomer* table, and we can create a foreign key (FK) on same field: *CustomerID* column in *TblOrder* table. Foreign key plays an important role to enforce data integrity (referential) in making sure that that *CustomerID* value entered in *TblOrder* table must exist in primary table: *TblCustomer* and if that customer is not existing in *TblCustomer*, SQL Server will display an error message. Therefore, foreign key helps in prevention of entry of wrong data and hence maintaining integrity of data inside SQL Server 2012 RDBMS.

A good coding practice is to add proper comments for your SQL statements so that if you needed to refer back in future, you can remind yourself or other developers the purpose of those SQL statements. Also, it is considered a good practice to have proper comments for good maintainability. This will be elaborated in next Chapter 5.

Another good SQL practice for table design is to add following 4 columns in every table. But, for brevity's sake and not to deviate from too much from core task of schema design, adding these 4 columns has been avoided but if you want to add these 4 columns, you can do so.

1) CreatedBy: Varchar(25), Not-Null, Default value: *System Admin*
2) CreatedOn: DateTime, Not-Null, Default value: GETUTCDATE(): date time in **C**oordinated **U**niversal **T**ime, rather than using date time in local time zone.
3) LastUpdatedBy: Varchar(25), Not-Null, Default value: *System Admin*
4) LastUpdatedOn: DateTime, Not-Null, Default value: GETUTCDATE()

In next Chapter 5, we will formally run various types of SQL queries for adding, updating or deleting a record into a table and others, although, this chapter already briefly introduced some of the SQL queries.

## Chapter 5: T-SQL: DDL, DML, DQL, DCL, DTL

Just like we need English, German, French, Hindi, Japanese, or Chinese language or for that matter any foreign national language to communicate amongst the people of that nation, similarly, to communicate and talk to SQL Server database, we need a language and it is named as **SQL:** *Structured Query Language*. SQL is used for querying/fetching data stored in SQL Server, altering/modifying existing data and defining relational databases. SQL Server understands the SQL language and responds appropriately to SQL commands. SQL language has been standardized by **ANSI:** *American National Standards Institute,* however, there are many flavors of its implementation by many technology companies like Microsoft, Oracle, IBM, Sybase, Teradata, etc. to provide a strategic edge to their implementation by leveraging their underlying core technological strengths in enhancing performance and features and therefore attracting a larger users base. We mention major implementations as below:

a. **T-SQL:** Transact-**SQL** or simply T-SQL is Microsoft's version of SQL and used by SQL Server. Once SQL Server was released as an **Express** and **free** edition by Microsoft for development purpose, SQL Server database has found ever growing user base in all category of companies: small or big. You still need to buy licenses for production.

b. **PL/SQL:** **P**rocedural **L**anguage/SQL or simply PL/SQL is another popular implementation of SQL by Oracle who was an early pioneer in developing industrial grade RDBMS that can withstand heavy duty load of queries, data ware housing and datamarts.

c. **PL/pgSQL:** It is another proprietary implementation of SQL and used by *PostgreSQL*.

In order to better understand and to have a good mental map of different SQL commands, we will categorize them into following broad types.


## 5.1 DATA DEFINITION LANGUAGE (DDL)

*Data Definition Language*, DDL SQL commands are used to define or construct the structure of SQL objects like databases, tables, columns, indexes. They are formally elucidated below:

a. **CREATE:** We have already seen this DDL command in earlier Chapter 4 to create tables (TblCustomer, TblProduct, and TblOrder) and also to create database (IMS).

Go to Studio and click on **New Query** () icon OR press hot keys: **Ctrl + N** OR go to Studio's top menu bar and Click **New -> Query with Current Connection** and a new Query Editor will be displayed as in below Fig. Make sure **IMS** database is selected in the drop down list of databases in Studio's toolbar (OR run following SQL commands in just opened Query Editor: **USE IMS**, press **ENTER** key on your keyboard, type-in **GO** and press either **Execute** (looks like an exclamation sign) icon OR simply press **F5** key on keyboard to run the SQL command; meaning that USE IMS and GO statements should be on 2 separate lines of editor, otherwise, an error message will be displayed.

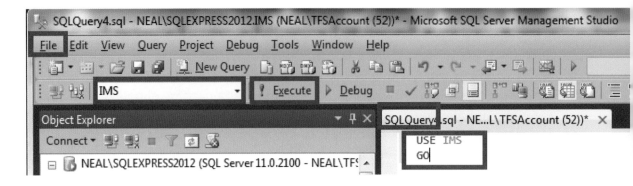

If the SQL command is successfully executed, you will see a message: *Command(s)* *completed successfully* in *Messages* window at the Studio's bottom.

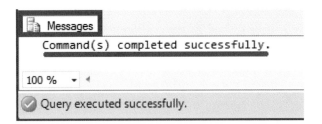

We will create a new test database **TEST.** Enter following T-SQL query to do so and press *F5* or click on *Execute* icon.

```
USE [master]
GO

CREATE DATABASE [Test]
CONTAINMENT = NONE
ON PRIMARY
(NAME = N'Test', FILENAME = N'c:\Program Files\Microsoft SQL
Server\MSSQL11.SQLEXPRESS2012\MSSQL\DATA\Test.mdf', SIZE = 3072KB,
MAXSIZE = UNLIMITED, FILEGROWTH = 1024KB)
LOG ON
(NAME = N'Test_log', FILENAME = N'c:\Program Files\Microsoft SQL
Server\MSSQL11.SQLEXPRESS2012\MSSQL\DATA\Test_log.ldf', SIZE = 1024KB,
MAXSIZE = 2048GB , FILEGROWTH = 10%)
GO
```

A new database should be displayed under Databases node in Object Explorer and if not, refresh it by Right Click on *Databases* node -> *Refresh.* Note that, SQL Server adds a new entry inside *master* database for the newly added test database to manage it comprehensively.

Now, enter following T-SQL query for creating a simple test table in **IMS** database along with a primary key and press *F5* key or click on *Execute* icon and you will see another successful completion message indicating that CREATE SQL command ran fine. In case there is any error, make sure that you entered the correct syntax.

```
USE IMS
GO
CREATE TABLE TblTest
(
    TestID INT,
    TestName VARCHAR(50),
    TestDate DATE NOT NULL,
    PRIMARY KEY (TestID)
)
```

A new table is added to the **IMS** database with the columns as defined above.

b. **ALTER**: It is used for changing the structure of a SQL object, as follows:
   1. Add a new *column TestPrice* to an existing table:
      ```
      ALTER TABLE TblTest
      ADD TestPrice DECIMAL(9,2)
      ```

   2. Add a new *constraint*, e.g., all the price of items need to be assigned a default value of $1.00 to begin with:
      ```
      ALTER TABLE TblTest
      ADD CONSTRAINT DF_TblTest_TestPrice DEFAULT 1.00 FOR TestPrice
      ```

   3. Add a new *column + constraint* together, means performing above Steps1 & 2 into a single SQL command. Note that constraint name is auto-assigned by SQL server, as compared to the specific constraint name (DF_TblTest_TestPrice) that we assigned in Step 2.
      ```
      ALTER TABLE TblTest
      ADD TestPrice DECIMAL(9,2) DEFAULT 1.00
      ```

   4. Add an index on a column using the following DDL statement:
      ```
      CREATE INDEX TblTest_IDX ON TblTest(TestName)
      ```

   5. Change the column definition, e.g., you may want to change the size of an existing column *TestName* from 50 characters max length to 100 chars:
      ```
      ALTER TABLE TblTest
      ALTER COLUMN TestName VARCHAR(100)
      ```

c. **RENAME:** A column in a table can be renamed using a stored procedure: sp_RENAME, but, we will discuss about it in details in Chapter 9.
   ```
   sp_RENAME 'TblTest.TestPrice','TestPriceNew','COLUMN'
   ```

Note that some RDBMS like Oracle does support *RENAME* SQL command.

d. **DROP:** It is used to drop/delete SQL objects: database, table, index, etc.

1. Drop a *Constraint*: *DF_Tbl_TestPrice* that we added in step b2:

```
ALTER TABLE [dbo].[TblTest]
DROP CONSTRAINT [DF_TblTest_TestPrice]
```

2. Drop a column: *TestPriceNew* field:

```
ALTER TABLE TblTest
DROP COLUMN TestPriceNew
```

Note that if you have a constraint on a field, it needs to be deleted *first* before you can delete the column itself and if you have a foreign key (FK) constraint or any other constraint, then, you would need to delete FK constraint first, otherwise, you get an error message:

```
The object 'DF_TblTest_TestPrice' is dependent on column 'TestPriceNew'.
ALTER TABLE DROP COLUMN TestPriceNew failed because one or more objects
access this column.
```

3. Drop a Table: DDL command to delete a table *completely,* note that table structure *along with data* will be deleted. So, you need to be careful before running this command, it is recommended to take a back-up of at-least table schema and save into local machine, before any *drop* SQL commands.

```
DROP TABLE TblTest
```

Note: You can use block quotes (**[...]**) around database, table, column names and it is recommended to use it as a good coding practice and also due to the fact that some of SQL reserved keywords will not be recognized without these block quotes. *We did not use them earlier due to keeping things simple, but, from now, as a matter of practice, we will always use block quotes.*

```
DROP TABLE [TblTest]
```

4. Drop a database: Earlier we created a test database and want to delete it completely; all the tables contained in this database along with data will be deleted with this SQL command.

```
USE [master]
GO
DROP DATABASE [Test]
GO
```

**NOTE:** *Only run this SQL DML command on a test database, otherwise, you will need to recreate database.*

e.  **TRUNCATE:** It is used for removing all the records from a table but without creating logging details. Since logging is not performed, so, all the records are deleted from table must faster and efficiently, but, note that you cannot retrieve the records once truncated from a table. So, you need to run this command carefully.

```
TRUNCATE TABLE [TblTest]
```

Note that *only* the data contained in a table will be deleted and table structure will still be remaining.

## 5.2 DATA MANIPULATION LANGUAGE (DML)

*Data Manipulation Language,* DML SQL commands are used primarily to add, insert or delete record/records, so called **CRUD** operations: *CR*eate, *U*pdate and *D*elete data tasks.

a.  **INSERT:** Add a new record to *TblTest* table:

```
INSERT INTO [dbo].[TblTest]
    (
      [TestID]
    ,[TestName]
    ,[TestDate]
    ,[TestPrice]
      )
VALUES
    (
      1
    ,'Book'
    ,'11-01-2013'
    ,10.00
      )
```

One record with above data will be populated in *TblTest* table. You can query this table using DQL as mentioned in next Step 3.

b.  **UPDATE:** Update the above added record, if you want to update the price of book from $10.00 to $11:50:

```
UPDATE [dbo].[TblTest]
    SET
      [TestPrice] = 11.50
WHERE TestID = 1
```

Note that you want to be careful while updating existing record or records, and generally want to add a **WHERE** clause, otherwise, all rows will be updated with price of 11.50.

c.  **DELETE:** Delete the newly added record:

```
DELETE FROM [dbo].[TblTest]
      WHERE TestID = 1
```

While running *delete* DML queries, you may want to write WHERE clause first and then delete statement, since, if you pressed accidently **F5** after writing *delete* query**,** all the records from table will be deleted. This style has found to save lot of headaches latter on as you do not to hear from folks that all useful data is gone. Another recommended practice is to comment out *delete* the SQL query as soon as you are done, so that you do not accidently run it again by mistake later. Normally, you want to highlight the SQL query (using SHIFT + Arrow down keys together) and click on **Execute** or **F5** to run a specific SQL query written in Query Editor.

In case you really want to delete or clean up all the data in a table and do it faster, *truncate* SQL command can be used. But, *truncate* cannot be used for deleting a single record or a specific set of records from a table, meaning that *delete* provides a finer granularity.

## 5.3 DATA QUERY LANGUAGE (DQL)

***Data Query Language,*** this DQL command is used to fetch/query the data from a table and you will be using this SQL command frequently to view the data stored in a table.

a. **SELECT ALL**: Get all the records from *TblTest* table:
```
SELECT * FROM [TblTest]
```
Note that * here means that data in *all* the columns are fetched, however, if you want to get data for some columns, you can specify those columns for which you need data. Note that providing exact column names is another good SQL coding practice and by doing so, SQL Server allows to run DQL command much faster since optimizer does not need to do a lookup for column names and just need to bring data for those specified columns only and not all data.
```
SELECT [TestID]
      ,[TestName]
      ,[TestDate]
FROM [TblTest]
```

b. **SELECT DISTINCT**: Get all the unique records, where all the column names are different for each record, means that rows fetched should not contain duplicate rows:
```
SELECT DISTINCT * FROM [TblTest]
```

c. **SELECT TOP**: Get first n rows from a table where n is an integer number, e.g., get first 10 rows from TblTest table:
```
SELECT TOP 10 * FROM [tblTest]
```

d. **SELECT WHERE**: Get all the *TestName* from TblTest table that have value as Bill:
```
SELECT * FROM [TblTest]
WHERE TestName = 'Book'
```

Note that **WHERE** clause is used to filter or narrow down the selection of rows.

If you want to get all the TestName that start with letter B, like Book, Bill, etc.
```
SELECT * FROM [TblTest]
```

```
WHERE TestName LIKE 'B%'
```

**%** sign is known as wild card character and any row that contains *TestName* starting with B will be returned in result set.

e. **SELECT ORDER BY**: Get all the rows with *TestName* displayed in ascending order of alphabets:
```
SELECT * FROM [TblTest]
ORDER BY TestName ASC
```

***ORDER BY*** clause is used to perform the sorting of the data returned and you can sort by single or multiple columns. Ascending is the default sort order, but, if you want to get rows in descending order, use ***ORDER BY DESC***.

## 5.4 DATA CONTROL LANGUAGE (DCL)

***Data Control Language,*** this DCL query is used to allocate privileges to a user or login or group on some database object. The purpose of granting specific permissions/ privileges is to maintain an appropriate level of security of the database objects and control access to these database objects to the right personnel.

a. **GRANT**: Grant privileges to select, insert, update, and delete data from *TblTest* table to a user: *TestUser*
```
-- First create a TestLogin with password 'password'
CREATE LOGIN TestLogin
    WITH PASSWORD = 'password'
GO


-- Add a database user for the login created above
CREATE USER TestUser FOR LOGIN TestLogin
GO


-- Now grant privileges to TestUser
GRANT SELECT, INSERT, UPDATE, DELETE ON [TblTest] TO TestUser
```

In order to help enforce security controls, typically, *roles* are first created and then users are assigned to belong to these roles, which help in avoiding having to assign individual permissions to individual users for each database objects.
```
-- Create a Role DEV
CREATE ROLE DEV
GO


-- Grant privileges to DEV Role
GRANT CREATE TABLE, INSERT, UPDATE, DELETE TO DEV
GO


-- Grant DEV role to TestUser
GRANT DEV TO TestUser
```

```
GO
```

b. **REVOKE**: Rescind/take back *delete* privileges from *TestUser* for database object *TblTest*:
```
-- Take back delete privileges from TestUser
REVOKE DELETE ON [TblTest] FROM TestUser
GO
```
Similarly, you can revoke *delete* privileges from *TestUser,* this time using *DEV* role:
```
REVOKE DELETE FROM DEV
GO
```

## 5.5 DATA TRANSACTION LANGUAGE (DTL)

***Data Transaction Language,*** also known as ***TCL, Transactional Control Language,*** DTL/TCL SQL commands are used to control transactions that are taking place inside a database. A transaction is a unit of work that results from DML SQL query/queries.

a. **BEGIN & COMMIT TRANSACTION:** A transaction starts with ***BEGIN TRANSACTION*** statement that delineates a start of SQL commands and its completion with ***COMMIT TRANSACTION.*** A transaction can consist of a single SQL command or several commands. Either *all* the SQL commands within a transaction are executed successfully or all of them do not finish, there is no in-between state where some SQL commands complete and others do not.

```
BEGIN TRANSACTION T1
        -- Update existing record
        UPDATE [dbo].[TblTest]
        SET
              [TestPrice] = 11.00
        WHERE TestID = 1

COMMIT TRANSACTION T1
```

Instead of fully spelling out ***TRANSACTION*** word above, SQL Server allows to use a short-hand notation: ***TRAN.*** Also, note that we attached [dbo] before a table name which refers to the ***d**ata**b**ase **o**wner schema to which *TblTest* belongs to. You can create other schema names and place tables in those schemas. Schema helps in assigning access permissions to users based on schema, rather than each individual table or other database objects. *T1* is the assigned name of transaction and it is not necessary to specify it but comes handy during rollback of transactions.

Also, semicolon (;) can be used after each SQL command as a separator, though, it is not necessary, as we have not used it so far but, some developers prefer to use them as a visual clue and it's a personal choice.

b. **MARKED TRANSACTIONS**: Marked transaction allows the name of transaction to be added in transaction log and hence, *MARKED* transaction becomes useful during restoration of database:
```
BEGIN TRANSACTION M1 WITH MARK
```

```
UPDATE [IMS].[dbo].[TblTest]
SET
        [TestPrice] = 11.00
WHERE TestID = 1

SELECT * from TblTest

COMMIT TRANSACTION M1
```

c. **NESTED TRANSACTIONS**: As name says, when you include one or more transactions within a transaction, it is known as *nested transactions.* For e.g., we can combine 2 transactions in above Steps 5a and 5b as below:

```
BEGIN TRANSACTION T1
        -- Update existing record
        UPDATE [IMS].[dbo].[TblTest]
        SET
                [TestPrice] = 11.00
        WHERE TestID = 1

        -- Nested transaction within T1 transaction
        BEGIN TRANSACTION M1 WITH MARK
                UPDATE [IMS].dbo].[TblTest]
                SET
                        [TestPrice] = 11.00
                WHERE TestID = 1

                SELECT * from TblTest

        COMMIT TRANSACTION M1;
COMMIT TRANSACTION T1
```

If any one of the inner transaction is rolled back, all the transactions, including the outer-most transaction will be rolled back. With the start (*begin*) of each transaction, **@@TRANCOUNT** value increments by 1, and with each *commit,* value decrements by 1.

d. **DISTRIBUTED TRANSACTION**: In case you have transactions that need to be run across multiple database servers, a *distributed transaction* is used:
```
BEGIN DISTRIBUTED TRANSACTION
        -- Delete a record from TblTest table in database: IMS
        DELETE [IMS].[dbo].TblTest
                WHERE TestID = 1

        -- Delete a record on other database server instance: SERVER2
        DELETE [SERVER2].[IMS].[dbo].[TblTest]
                WHERE TestID = 2
COMMIT TRANSACTION
```

Note the use of 4 dots to specify: *DatabaseServerInstanceName. DatabaseCatalogName. SchemaName.TableName.*

e. **SAVEPOINT & ROLLBACK TRANSACTION**: You can set a marker or a point within a transaction and this is the point to which a transaction can roll back to, without rolling back complete transaction, or in other words, you can commit a part of complete transaction up to the *savepoint*. **SAVE TRAN** or **SAVE TRANSACTION** is used to create a *savepoint* and **ROLLBACK TRAN *savepoint-name*** is used to rollback a part of transaction up to the point where *savepoint* was created. You can create one or more than one *savepoints*.

```
PRINT @@TRANCOUNT
BEGIN TRANSACTION
        -- Update existing record
        UPDATE [IMS].[dbo].[TblTest]
        SET
                [TestPrice] = 12.00
        WHERE TestID  = 1


        -- Create a savepoint 1 at this point
        SAVE TRANSACTION SavePoint1


        -- Another SQL command
        UPDATE [IMS].[dbo].[TblTest]
        SET
                [TestPrice] = 15.00
        WHERE TestID  = 2


        SELECT * FROM [IMS].[dbo].[TblTest] ORDER BY TestID
        PRINT @@TRANCOUNT


        -- Rollback to savepoint SavePoint1
        ROLLBACK TRANSACTION SavePoint1

COMMIT TRANSACTION
PRINT @@TRANCOUNT
```

Once you run above SQL commands, you will notice that only first SQL *update* command holds, since, we rolled back up to savepoint 1 and therefore, 2nd SQL command was rolled back and only 1st SQL update is committed.

Note that value of **@@TRANCOUNT** is not changed due to **save transaction.**

## 5.5 COMMENTS: SINGLE AND MULTI LINE

**Comment:** You can add comments or description for the SQL commands for understanding the purpose of a column or any information about logic used and reasoning so that these comments can be referred later on by you or other developer who wants to understand a SQL object that you create. There are 2 forms of comments:

a. Single line comment: -- (double hyphens): when you prefix 2 hyphens before any text, it will be treated by SQL server as a remark and not an actual SQL command, e.g., notice that color of text changes to green, indicating that Studio treats it a *comment* and ignores as SQL command.

```
-- Delete the data in TblTest table withour actually deleting the table
-- Table Name TblTest
```

b. Multi-line comment: /*... */ (forward slash-asterisk ... asterisks forward slash): in case you have several lines, you can use this style, however, to keep consistency and esthetic reasons, we will to use above style (f1). As we said earlier, it does not matter which style you prefer to use or get as esoteric as you want, as long as consistency is maintained throughout coding.

```
/* Delete the data in TblTest table without actually deleting the table
   TblTest schema */
```

## 5.6 ERROR HANDLING

**Error Handling:** As we mentioned earlier that there are many times, when SQL queries could run into errors due to any number of reasons and SQL Server throws some default exception/error. As a good coding practice, it is recommended to catch the error and handle it appropriately with right messages. We use *TRY-CATCH* block in order to trap an error as below:

1. **TRY-CATCH**:

```
BEGIN TRY
    -- Create a datatype error
      UPDATE [dbo].[TblTest]
      SET
            [TestDate] = 2.0
      WHERE TestID  = 1
END TRY
BEGIN CATCH
    SELECT
        ERROR_NUMBER() AS ErrorNumber
      ,ERROR_MESSAGE() AS ErrorMessage
      ,ERROR_STATE() AS ErrorState
      ,ERROR_SEVERITY() AS ErrorSeverity
      ,ERROR_PROCEDURE() AS ErrorProcedure
      ,ERROR_LINE() AS ErrorLine
END CATCH;
```

Note that SQL is not case-sensitive meaning that you can write SQL commands in either small or capital letters and they would mean same command, e.g. INSERT or insert SQL command will perform same action inside SQL Server database or any other RDBMS.

Another good practice is to add proper comments for your SQL statements so that if you needed to refer back in future, you can remind yourself or other developers the purpose of those SQL statements. Also, it is considered a good practice to have proper comments for good maintainability.

In next Chapter 6, we will discuss various types of *joins* and in order to learn them, we first add following records into *TblCustomer, TblProduct* and *TblOrder* tables.

1. **TblCustomer**:

```sql
-- Delete all existing records in TblCustomer table so as to have clean
records
DELETE FROM [IMS].[dbo].[TblCustomer]

-- Turn on Identity insert for one time adding of data, along with
identity column value
SET IDENTITY_INSERT [IMS].[dbo].[TblCustomer] ON

INSERT INTO [IMS].[dbo].[TblCustomer]
([CustomerID],[FirstName],[MiddleName],[LastName],[Address],[City],[Sta
te],[ZipCode],[Phone],[Country])
VALUES (1, 'Melinda', '', 'Gates', '209 Highway', 'Seattle', 'WA',
'10001', '123-456-7890', 'USA')
INSERT INTO [IMS].[dbo].[TblCustomer]
([CustomerID],[FirstName],[MiddleName],[LastName],[Address],[City],[Sta
te],[ZipCode],[Phone],[Country])
VALUES (2, 'Jim', '', 'Cramer', '1230 Plano Rd.', 'New York', 'NY',
'10002', '223-456-7890', 'USA')
INSERT INTO [IMS].[dbo].[TblCustomer]
([CustomerID],[FirstName],[Middlename],[LastName],[Address],[City],[Sta
te],[ZipCode],[Phone],[Country])
VALUES (3, 'Larry', '', 'Page', '1 Larry Way', 'San Francisco', 'CA',
'10003', '323-456-7890', 'USA')
INSERT INTO [IMS].[dbo].[TblCustomer]
([CustomerID],[FirstName],[MiddleName],[LastName],[Address],[City],[Sta
te],[ZipCode],[Phone],[Country])
VALUES (4, 'Marion', '', 'Kerry', '4500 Dallas Rd', 'Dallas', 'TX',
'10004', '423-456-7890', 'USA')
INSERT INTO [IMS].[dbo].[TblCustomer]
([CustomerID],[FirstName],[MiddleName],[LastName],[Address],[City],[Sta
te],[ZipCode],[Phone],[Country])
VALUES (5, 'Mike', '', 'Henson', '100 Carrollton Rd', 'San Louis',
'MO', '10005', '523-456-7890', 'USA')

-- Turn off Identity column insert: back to original design schema
SET IDENTITY_INSERT [IMS].[dbo].[TblCustomer] OFF
```

2. **TblProduct**:

```sql
-- Turn on Identity insert for one time adding of data, along with
identity column value
SET IDENTITY_INSERT [IMS].[dbo].[TblProduct] ON
```

```
INSERT INTO [IMS].[dbo].[TblProduct]
([ProductID],[Name],[Description],[Manufacturer],[QtyAvailable],[Price]
)
VALUES (1,'SQLServer2012', 'MS SQL Server 2012', 'Microsoft', 10,
5000.00)
INSERT INTO [IMS].[dbo].[TblProduct]
([ProductID],[Name],[Description],[Manufacturer],[QtyAvailable],[Price]
)
VALUES (2,'Lumia900', 'Windows 8 Smart Phone', 'Nokia', 15, 495.00)
INSERT INTO [IMS].[dbo].[TblProduct]
([ProductID],[Name],[Description],[Manufacturer],[QtyAvailable],[Price]
)
VALUES (3,'KindleHDX', 'Tablet Device', 'Amazon', 20, 299.00)
INSERT INTO [IMS].[dbo].[TblProduct]
([ProductID],[Name],[Description],[Manufacturer],[QtyAvailable],[Price]
)
VALUES (4,'iPhone5S', 'Apple Smart Phone', 'Apple', 25, 650.00)
INSERT INTO [IMS].[dbo].[TblProduct]
([ProductID],[Name],[Description],[Manufacturer],[QtyAvailable],[Price]
)
VALUES (5,'GoogleGlass', 'Google Smart Glass', 'Google', 5, 1500.00)

-- Turn off Identity column insert: back to original design schema
SET IDENTITY_INSERT [IMS].[dbo].[TblProduct] OFF
```

3. **TblOrder**:

```
-- Delete all existing records so as to have clean records
DELETE FROM [IMS].[dbo].[TblOrder]

-- Turn on Identity insert for one time adding of data, along with
identity column value
SET IDENTITY_INSERT [IMS].[dbo].[TblOrder] ON
INSERT INTO [IMS].[dbo].[TblOrder] ([OrderID],[CustomerID],
[ProductID],[OrderQty],[OrderDate],[IsOrderActive],[Comment])
VALUES (1, 1, 1, 1, '2013-11-29', 0, 'Delivered')
INSERT INTO [IMS].[dbo].[TblOrder] ([OrderID],[CustomerID],
[ProductID],[OrderQty],[OrderDate],[IsOrderActive],[Comment])
VALUES (2, 2, 2, 2, '2013-11-29', 0, 'Delivered')
INSERT INTO [IMS].[dbo].[TblOrder] ([OrderID],[CustomerID],
[ProductID],[OrderQty],[OrderDate],[IsOrderActive],[Comment])
VALUES (3, 3, 3, 3, '2013-11-29', 0, 'Delivered')
INSERT INTO [IMS].[dbo].[TblOrder] ([OrderID],[CustomerID],
[ProductID],[OrderQty],[OrderDate],[IsOrderActive],[Comment])
VALUES (4, 4, 4, 4, '2013-11-29', 0, 'Delivered')
INSERT INTO [IMS].[dbo].[TblOrder] ([OrderID],[CustomerID],
[ProductID],[OrderQty],[OrderDate],[IsOrderActive],[Comment])
VALUES (5, 5, 5, 5, '2013-11-29', 1, 'Processing')

-- Turn off Identity column insert: back to original design schema
SET IDENTITY_INSERT [IMS].[dbo].[TblCustomer] OFF
```

## *Chapter 6: Joins: Inner, Left, Right, Cross, Self, Full, Natural and Theta*

In Chapters 4 and 5, we saw the creation of normalized tables: *TblCustomer, TblProduct and TblOrder* in **IMS** database. However, if we need to fetch records from two or more tables, you would need to use *joins*, e.g., if you need all the products ordered by a customer. *Join* between tables occurs using a common field between the tables, e.g., *ProductID* field can be used to join *TblProduct* and *TblOrder* tables. Joins provides a means to combines fields from two or more tables. There are several types of *joins* and they are elaborated below.

## 6.1 INNER JOIN

**INNER JOIN**: It is also known as **EQUI-JOIN** or simply as **JOIN** and allows fetching all the rows from the multiple tables, as long as there are matches (based on a common field) in both the tables, e.g., *TblOrder* table contains *CustomerID* field which identifies a customer who ordered the products and *TblCustomer* table also contains *CustomerID* and therefore, *CustomerID* is a common field amongst these 2 tables. So, we will join these 2 tables using CustomerID and fetch all orders along with their customers:

```
SELECT
    [TblOrder].[OrderID]
    ,[TblCustomer].[FirstName]
    ,[TblCustomer].[LastName]
    ,[TblOrder].[OrderQty]
    ,[TblOrder].[OrderDate]
    ,[TblOrder].[IsOrderActive]
    ,[TblOrder].[Comment]
FROM [IMS].[dbo].[TblOrder]
INNER JOIN [IMS].[dbo].[TblCustomer]
ON [TblOrder].[CustomerID] = [TblCustomer].[CustomerID]
```

You will be seeing following result set:

| OrderID | FirstName | LastName | OrderQty | OrderDate | IsOrderActive | Comment |
|---|---|---|---|---|---|---|
| 1 | Melinda | Gates | 1 | 11/29/13 0:00 | 0 | Delivered |
| 2 | Jim | Cramer | 2 | 11/29/13 0:00 | 0 | Delivered |
| 3 | Larry | Page | 3 | 11/29/13 0:00 | 0 | Delivered |
| 4 | Marion | Kerry | 4 | 11/29/13 0:00 | 0 | Delivered |
| 5 | Mike | Henson | 5 | 11/29/13 0:00 | 1 | Processing |

We normally assign an **alias** name to a table name in order to refer fields in a table, which helps in identifying each field selected and at the same time without having to type **full** table name each and every time, as below. Alias is really another name for a table and generally a short notation.

```
SELECT
     C.[FirstName]
    ,C.[LastName]
    ,O.[OrderID]

    ,O.[OrderQty]
    ,O.[OrderDate]
    ,O.[IsOrderActive]
    ,O.[Comment]
FROM [IMS].[dbo].[TblOrder] O
INNER JOIN [IMS].[dbo].[TblCustomer] C
ON O.[CustomerID] = C.[CustomerID]
```

Alias **O** represents table *TblOrder* and **C** stands for table *TblCustomer*. As you can see, above format is much more readable, faster to type-in and much more understandable. In case you need to get orders for a *CustomerID* = 1 only, you can add a **WHERE** clause at the end of above SQL command and only 1 record will be returned with the data that we have inserted in Chapter 5.

## 6.2 LEFT OUTER JOIN

**LEFT OUTER JOIN**: This join is also referred simply as **LEFT JOIN** and fetches **all** rows from the *left* table, even if there are no matches in the *right* table. In case the *right* table rows matches with *left* table (using a common joining field), matching data from *right* table is also returned, otherwise, it returns *NULL* values from *right* table.

```
SELECT
     O.[OrderID]
    ,C.[FirstName]
    ,C.[LastName]
    ,O.[OrderQty]
    ,O.[OrderDate]
    ,O.[IsOrderActive]
    ,O.[Comment]
FROM [IMS].[dbo].[TblCustomer] C
LEFT OUTER JOIN [IMS].[dbo].[TblOrder] O
ON O.[CustomerID] = C.[CustomerID]
```

Note that in above query, left table is *TblCustomer* and *TblOrder* is right table.

```
-- Turn on Identity insert for adding a new customer
SET IDENTITY_INSERT [IMS].[dbo].[TblCustomer] ON

INSERT INTO [IMS].[dbo].[TblCustomer]
([CustomerID],[FirstName],[MiddleName],[LastName],[Address],[City],[State],
[ZipCode],[Phone],[Country])
VALUES (6, 'Kevin', '', 'Costner', '100 Hudson Way', 'Houston', 'TX',
'10006', '623-456-7890', 'USA')
```

```
-- Turn off Identity column insert: back to original design schema
SET IDENTITY_INSERT [IMS].[dbo].[TblCustomer] OFF
```

If you add another new customer (CustomerID = 6, say) as above, who did not order any products, and run above query with **LEFT JOIN**, you will see that all 6 customers will be returned, however, field values for order row will have NULL values, since, CustomerID = 6 is not found *TblOrder* table.

| FirstName | LastName | OrderID | OrderQty | OrderDate | IsOrderActive | Comment |
|-----------|----------|---------|----------|-----------|---------------|---------|
| Melinda | Gates | 1 | 1 | 11/29/13 0:00 | 0 | Delivered |
| Jim | Cramer | 2 | 2 | 11/29/13 0:00 | 0 | Delivered |
| Larry | Page | 3 | 3 | 11/29/13 0:00 | 0 | Delivered |
| Marion | Kerry | 4 | 4 | 11/29/13 0:00 | 0 | Delivered |
| Mike | Henson | 5 | 5 | 11/29/13 0:00 | 1 | Processing |
| Kevin | Costner | *NULL* | *NULL* | *NULL* | *NULL* | *NULL* |

## 6.3 RIGHT OUTER JOIN

**RIGHT OUTER JOIN**: This join is also referred simply as **RIGHT JOIN** and fetches **all** rows from the *right* table, even if there are no matches in the *left* table. In case the *left* table rows matches with *right* table (using a common joining field), matching data from left table is also returned, otherwise, it returns *NULL* values from *left* table.

```
SELECT
        P.[ProductID]
        ,P.[Name]
        ,P.[Description]
        ,P.[Manufacturer]
        ,P.[QtyAvailable]
        ,P.[Price]
        ,O.[OrderID]
FROM [IMS].[dbo].[TblOrder] O
RIGHT OUTER JOIN [IMS].[dbo].[TblProduct] P
ON O.ProductID = P.ProductID
```

| ProductID | Name | Description | Manufacturer | QtyAvailable | Price | OrderID |
|-----------|------|-------------|--------------|--------------|-------|---------|
| 1 | SQLServer2012 | MS SQL Server 2012 | Microsoft | 10 | 5000 | 1 |
| 2 | Lumia900 | Windows 8 Smart Phone | Nokia | 15 | 495 | 2 |
| 3 | KindleHDX | Tablet Device | Amazon | 20 | 299 | 3 |
| 4 | iPhone5S | Apple Smart Phone | Apple | 25 | 650 | 4 |
| 5 | GoogleGlass | Google Smart Glass | Google | 5 | 1500 | 5 |
| 6 | GECafeCooktop | Gas Cooktop | General | 2 | 1000 | *NULL* |

| | | | | Electric | | | |
|---|---|---|---|---|---|---|---|

Notice in result set above, although all 6 rows from *TblProduct* table (*right*) are display 6th customer, however, since, no matching order for ProductID = 6 was found in TblOrder table (left), it is returned as *NULL*.

## 6.4 FULL OUTER JOIN

**FULL OUTER JOIN**: This join is also referred simply as **FULL JOIN** and fetches rows that are combination of above 2 joins: **LEFT JOIN** and **RIGHT JOIN,** meaning that it returns rows from both tables whenever there are matches (on common joining field) and returns *NULL* values when the rows do not match.

```
SELECT
        P.[ProductID]
        ,P.[Name]
        ,P.[Description]
        ,P.[Manufacturer]
        ,P.[QtyAvailable]
        ,P.[Price]
        ,O.[OrderID]
FROM [IMS].[dbo].[TblProduct] P
FULL OUTER JOIN [IMS].[dbo].[TblOrder] O
ON O.ProductID = P.ProductID
```

## 6.5 CROSS JOIN

**CROSS JOIN**: This join is also known as **CARTESIAN JOIN,** and fetches combinations of rows from left table and right table (Cartesian product) and if there are many rows in both table, may result in lot of rows and sometimes bogging down or crashing al-together a system.

```
SELECT
        P.[ProductID]
        ,P.[Name]
        ,P.[Description]
        ,P.[Manufacturer]
        ,P.[QtyAvailable]
        ,P.[Price]
        ,O.[OrderID]
FROM [IMS].[dbo].[TblOrder] O
CROSS JOIN [IMS].[dbo].[TblProduct] P
```

The result set of above SQL will be 30 rows (6 Products x 5 Orders = 30 combinations).

## 6.6 NATURAL JOIN

**NATURAL JOIN**: This is almost similar to **EQUI-JOIN** except that same/duplicate columns are not returned. SQL Server does not have NATURAL JOIN syntactically however Oracle does have it, although, there are ways to get the behavior of *natural join* in SQL Server using **INNER JOIN**.

## 6.7 SELF-JOIN

**SELF-JOIN**: It is similar to *INNER* OR *OUTER* JOIN, but, it joins a table to itself, instead of other tables. A typical example for self-join is when you need to fetch the name of manager of an employee where there is only one table: *TblEmployee* that contains entire employee IDs, names of employees, along with their manager ID. This can be achieved by using a *SELF-JOIN* as below:

First create an employee table as below:

```
CREATE TABLE [IMS].[dbo].[TblEmployee]
(
    [EmployeeID] [int] IDENTITY(1,1) NOT NULL,
    [FirstName] [varchar](50) NOT NULL,
    [LastName] [varchar](50) NOT NULL,
    [Address] [varchar](200) NULL,
    [City] [varchar](50) NULL,
    [State] [varchar](25) NULL,
    [ZipCode] [varchar](10) NULL,
    [ManagerID] [int] NULL,
    CONSTRAINT [PK_TblEmployee] PRIMARY KEY CLUSTERED (
    [EmployeeID] ASC
    )WITH (PAD_INDEX = OFF, STATISTICS_NORECOMPUTE = OFF, IGNORE_DUP_KEY =
    OFF, ALLOW_ROW_LOCKS = ON, ALLOW_PAGE_LOCKS = ON) ON [PRIMARY]
) ON [PRIMARY]
```

Now, insert following employees and get the name of manager as below:

```
-- Turn on Identity insert for adding employee
SET IDENTITY_INSERT [IMS].[dbo].[TblEmployee] ON

INSERT INTO [IMS].[dbo].[TblEmployee]
([EmployeeID],[FirstName],[LastName],[Address],[City],[State],[ZipCode],[M
anagerID])
VALUES (1,'Jay','Conard','123 State Hwy','Dallas','TX','12345', 2)
INSERT INTO [IMS].[dbo].[TblEmployee]
([EmployeeID],[FirstName],[LastName],[Address],[City],[State],[ZipCode],[M
anagerID])
VALUES (2,'George','Shultz','123 State Hwy','Houston','TX','22345', NULL)

-- Turn off Identity insert
SET IDENTITY_INSERT [IMS].[dbo].[TblEmployee] OFF


SELECT
    EMP1.EmployeeID
    ,EMP1.FirstName
    ,EMP1.Address
    ,EMP1.City
```

```
    ,EMP1.State
    ,EMP1.ZipCode
FROM [IMS].[dbo].[TblEmployee] EMP1, [IMS].[dbo].[TblEmployee] EMP2
WHERE EMP1.EmployeeID = EMP2.ManagerID
```

## 6.8 THETA JOIN

**THETA JOIN**: This join is similar to *EQUI-JOIN*, except that it allows other operators like >, >=, <, etc.

In next Chapter 7, we will discuss about indexes and how they can be used for improving performance.

## Chapter 7: Indexes: Unique, Clustered, Non-Clustered, Composite, Filtered, Covering

To better understand indexes and why we need them, let's take an example of book and say you were looking for info on some topic. There are two ways to look up that info in book:

    a.  1st option is to go over page by page and check if the topic exists and keep doing it till you find the topic of interest.

    b.  2nd option is to go to the list of topic index at the back of book, find topic of interest, get page number listed and go directly to that page.

### 7.1 TABLE SCAN AND TABLE SEEK

The 2nd approach is much-2 faster as compared to 1st one, especially, if the book happens to contain lot of pages. Similarly, if you need to search a record, e.g., a Customer with a last name, inside a table, SQL Server can perform a comparison record by record and see it matches with what you were searching for. If there are millions of rows, it will take a significant amount of time to search all the rows in table until the record is found. This searching of rows in a table one record at a time is referred to *scanning* of table or simply **TABLE SCAN**, which is time consuming operation.

Now, using the 2nd approach, if we similarly add an *index* that points to the record in a table that you were looking for, it is going to be much faster as compared to full table scan and that's reason why we add an *index* to a table for faster retrieval of data. This is also referred as *seeking* of data in a table or simply **TABLE SEEK**. So, *table seek* (option 2) is faster than *table scan* (option 1).

Note that Index is physically stored on the disk and organized as B-Tree structure that has a **root node** at the top, and at the bottom are **leaf nodes** and in between nodes are **intermediate leafs** which really point to leaf node.

We will demonstrate it with an example as below:

    a.  Drop existing *TblEmployee* table, re-create *TblEmployee* table (without index first), add some records and review execution plan:

```
DROP TABLE [IMS].[dbo].[TblEmployee]

CREATE TABLE [IMS].[dbo].[TblEmployee](
    [EmployeeID] [int] IDENTITY(1,1) NOT NULL,
    [FirstName] [varchar](50) NOT NULL,
    [LastName] [varchar](50) NOT NULL,
    [Address] [varchar](200) NULL,
    [City] [varchar](50) NULL,
    [State] [varchar](25) NULL,
    [ZipCode] [varchar](10) NULL,
    [ManagerID] [int] NULL,
```

```
)

-- Turn on Identity insert for adding employee
SET IDENTITY_INSERT [IMS].[dbo].[TblEmployee] ON

INSERT INTO [IMS].[dbo].[TblEmployee]
([EmployeeID],[FirstName],[LastName],[Address],[City],[State],[ZipCode],[M
anagerID])
VALUES (1,'Jay','Conard','123 State Hwy','Dallas','TX','12345', 2)
INSERT INTO [IMS].[dbo].[TblEmployee]
([EmployeeID],[FirstName],[LastName],[Address],[City],[State],[ZipCode],[M
anagerID])
VALUES (2,'George','Shultz','123 State Hwy','Houston','TX','22345', NULL)

-- Turn off Identity insert
SET IDENTITY_INSERT [IMS].[dbo].[TblEmployee] OFF
```

b. Click on image ( ) in toolbar of Studio that allows to **Include Actual Execution Plan** and execute following SQL statement:

```
SELECT * FROM [IMS].[dbo].[TblEmployee]
WHERE EmployeeID = 1
```

You will be seeing *Execution Plan* tab along with *Results* and *Messages* in bottom output window of Studio. Notice that above SQL statement performed a *table scan* (not table seek, since, index was not existing yet).

If you hover over the above blue high-lighted *Table Scan* rectangular box, you will be seeing details about the table scan as in below Fig., most importantly:
   1. *Physical Operation*: Table scan or table seek
   2. *Actual Number of Rows*: Rows returned
   3. *Estimated Subtree Cost*: time taken to perform search in B-Tree structure
   4. *Estimated Row Size*: Bytes size of returned data
   5. *Ordered*: True or False
   6. *Object*: Name of table
   7. *Output List*: Fields names

**Table Scan**

Scan rows from a table.

| | |
|---|---|
| Physical Operation | Table Scan |
| Logical Operation | Table Scan |
| Actual Execution Mode | Row |
| Estimated Execution Mode | Row |
| Actual Number of Rows | 3 |
| Actual Number of Batches | 0 |
| Estimated I/O Cost | 0.0032035 |
| Estimated Operator Cost | 0.0032853 (100%) |
| Estimated CPU Cost | 0.0000818 |
| Estimated Subtree Cost | 0.0032853 |
| Estimated Number of Executions | 1 |
| Number of Executions | 1 |
| Estimated Number of Rows | 3 |
| Estimated Row Size | 221 B |
| Actual Rebinds | 0 |
| Actual Rewinds | 0 |
| Ordered | False |
| Node ID | 0 |

Object
[IMS].[dbo].[TblEmployee]
Output List
[IMS].[dbo].[TblEmployee].EmployeeID, [IMS].[dbo].
[TblEmployee].FirstName, [IMS].[dbo].
[TblEmployee].LastName, [IMS].[dbo].
[TblEmployee].Address, [IMS].[dbo].[TblEmployee].City,
[IMS].[dbo].[TblEmployee].State, [IMS].[dbo].
[TblEmployee].ZipCode, [IMS].[dbo].

Now, we will see different indexes and execution plan will be mentioned as below.

## 7.2 CLUSTERED INDEX

**CLUSTERED INDEX**: We will first mention the steps that can be used to create a clustered index using the Studio and then using SQL statement.

a. Go to **Studio** -> Expand **IMS** node under **Databases** -> Expand **Tables** node -> Expand **TblEmployee** node -> Right Click on **Indexes** node -> Select **New Index** -> Select **Clustered Index...**
b. Click on **Add...** -> Select EmployeeID column as shown in below Fig.
c. Enter the name of index: *IX_TblEmployee_EmployeeID* in **Index Name** as shown in below Fig. Prefix **IX** stands for *an IndeX*. Note that there are many variations of naming an index but to keep things simple for now, we will stick to *IX* prefix convention.
d. Press **OK** and you will see *clustered index* listed under **Indexes** node.

Notice that, there is a check mark box under Clustered in **New Index** message box and if you put a check, it will make this clustered index as *unique clustered index*.

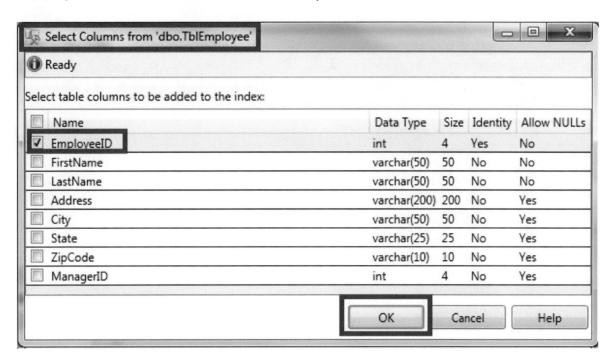

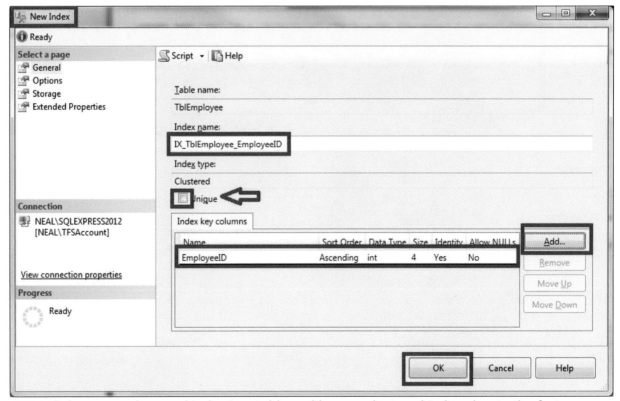

You can only have *one* clustered index in a table, unlike non-clustered index, due to the fact that table can be sorted in only in ascending or descending order of the column values and stored on disk physically only in one way.

A clustered index can also be alternatively created by running below SQL statement:

```
-- Drop the clustered index that was created with Studio
DROP INDEX [IX_TblEmployee_EmployeeID] ON [dbo].[TblEmployee]

CREATE CLUSTERED INDEX [IX_TblEmployee_EmployeeID]
ON [IMS].[dbo].[TblEmployee]
(
    [EmployeeID] ASC
)
```

Now, run the same SQL command to fetch the employees:

```
SELECT * FROM [IMS].[dbo].[TblEmployee]
WHERE EmployeeID = 1
```

Now, notice the difference in *execution plan* and it shows that above query is now using clustered index, though the *Estimated Subtree Cost* is less than earlier. Notice that it is using *table scan*, implemented via *clustered index*.

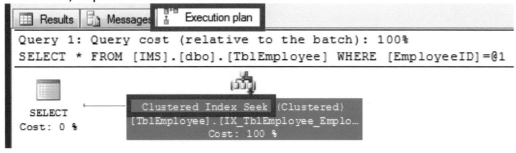

```
┌─────────────────────────────────────────┐
│  Clustered Index Seek (Clustered)        │
└─────────────────────────────────────────┘
Scanning a particular range of rows from a clustered index.
```

| | |
|---|---|
| **Physical Operation** | Clustered Index Seek |
| **Logical Operation** | Clustered Index Seek |
| **Actual Execution Mode** | Row |
| **Estimated Execution Mode** | Row |
| **Storage** | RowStore |
| **Actual Number of Rows** | 1 |
| **Actual Number of Batches** | 0 |
| **Estimated Operator Cost** | 0.0032831 (100%) |
| **Estimated I/O Cost** | 0.003125 |
| **Estimated CPU Cost** | 0.0001581 |
| **Estimated Subtree Cost** | 0.0032831 |
| **Number of Executions** | 1 |
| **Estimated Number of Executions** | 1 |
| **Estimated Number of Rows** | 1 |
| **Estimated Row Size** | 221 B |
| **Actual Rebinds** | 0 |
| **Actual Rewinds** | 0 |
| **Ordered** | True |
| **Node ID** | 0 |

## 7.3 NON-CLUSTERED INDEX

**NON-CLUSTERED INDEX**: Similar to above steps, we will first create a non-clustered index using Studio and then SQL statement:

a. Go to **Studio** -> Expand **IMS** node under **Databases** -> Expand **Tables** node -> Expand **TblEmployee** node -> Right Click on **Indexes** node -> Select **New Index** -> Select **Non-Clustered Index...**

b. Click on **Add...** -> Select EmployeeID column as shown in below Fig.

c. Enter the name of index: *IX_TblEmployee_FirstName* in **Index Name**.

d. Press **OK** and you will see *non-clustered index* listed under **Indexes** node.

Notice that, there is a check mark box under Non Clustered in **New Index** message box and if you put a check, it will make this non-clustered index as *unique non-clustered index*.

Now, if you run following SQL query and check the execution plan, it will show that it is using non-clustered index.

```
-- Drop the non-clustered index that was created with Studio
DROP INDEX [IX_TblEmployee_FirstName] ON [dbo].[TblEmployee]

CREATE NONCLUSTERED INDEX [IX_TblEmployee_FirstName]
ON [IMS].[dbo].[TblEmployee]
(
    [FirstName] ASC
)
```

```
-- We use a hint to use non-clustered index, otherwise, SQL Server ignores
it as table is small
SELECT * FROM [IMS].[dbo].[TblEmployee]
WITH(INDEX(IX_TblEmployee_FirstName))
WHERE FirstName = 'Jay'
```

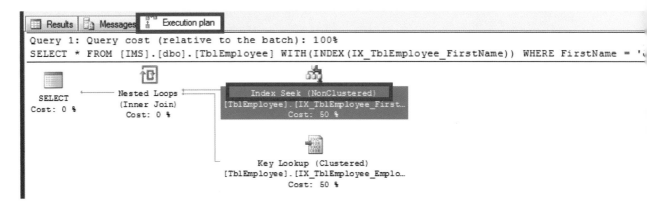

As you can see in above execution plan, both the indexes are used, since, data is not stored
at leaf-level (that we hinted to use non-clustered index) but rather SQL query has to go
clustered index to fetch it, where it is stored.

### Index Seek (NonClustered)

Scan a particular range of rows from a nonclustered
index.

| | |
|---|---|
| **Physical Operation** | Index Seek |
| **Logical Operation** | Index Seek |
| **Actual Execution Mode** | Row |
| **Estimated Execution Mode** | Row |
| **Storage** | RowStore |
| **Actual Number of Rows** | 1 |
| **Actual Number of Batches** | 0 |
| **Estimated Operator Cost** | 0.0032835 (50%) |
| **Estimated I/O Cost** | 0.003125 |
| **Estimated CPU Cost** | 0.0001585 |
| **Estimated Subtree Cost** | 0.0032835 |

There can be only one clustered index in a table as explained earlier; however, you can
create more than one non-clustered index and up to 256.

## 7.4 UNIQUE INDEXES

**UNIQUE INDEX**: You can create either *UNIQUE CLUSTERED INDEX* OR *UNIQUE NON-
CLUSTERED INDEX* where the column for each row can store only *unique* values. As was
explained earlier above, if you put a check, it will create appropriate unique indexes.

Now, we will be using SQL statements to create these unique indexes:

```
-- Drop the existing clustered index
DROP INDEX [IX_TblEmployee_EmployeeID] ON [dbo].[TblEmployee]

-- Drop the existing non-clustered index
DROP INDEX [IX_TblEmployee_FirstName] ON [dbo].[TblEmployee]

-- Create a unique clustered index
CREATE UNIQUE CLUSTERED INDEX [IX_TblEmployee_EmployeeID]
ON [IMS].[dbo].[TblEmployee]
(
    [EmployeeID] ASC
)

-- Create a unique non-clustered index
CREATE UNIQUE NONCLUSTERED INDEX [IX_TblEmployee_FirstName]
ON [IMS].[dbo].[TblEmployee]
(
    [FirstName] ASC
)
```

## 7.5 MULTI-COLUMN INDEX

**MULTI-COLUMN INDEX**: So far we created indexes that were based on single column. However, if the index is created with more than 1 column, it is referred as *multi-column index* as below. Sometimes, it is referred to as **COMPOSITE INDEX**.

```
CREATE NONCLUSTERED INDEX [IX_TblEmployee_FirstName_LastName] ON
[IMS].[dbo].[TblEmployee]
(
    [FirstName], [LastName]
)
```

## 7.6 IMPLICIT INDEX

**IMPLICIT INDEX**: Some indexes are automatically created by SQL server, e.g., when you create a Primary Key (PK), it will generally create a clustered index, unless explicitly stated otherwise and a *Unique Constraint* creates a *Non-Clustered Index*.

## 7.7 FILTERED INDEX

**FILTERED INDEX**: A *filtered index* is really a non-clustered index that operates on a subset of data, e.g., index to select a narrow range of rows that are not NULL and can greatly improve performance of query and being on a smaller set of data, helps in reducing disk space requirement and hence faster index maintenance, due to smaller footprint.

a. Go to **Studio** -> Expand **IMS** node under **Databases** -> Expand **Tables** node -> Expand **TblEmployee** node -> Right Click on **Indexes** node -> Select **New Index** -> Select **Non-Clustered Index...**
b. Click on **Add...** -> Check **City** column from **Select Columns from dbo.TblEmployee**.
c. Enter the name of index: *IX_TblEmployee_City* in **Index Name**.

d.  Under **Select a page,** choose **Filter** page and enter the *Filter Expression: City IS NOT NULL.*

e.  Press **OK** and you will see *filtered index* listed under **Indexes** node.

Alternatively, you can run following SQL commands to create a filtered index by first dropping index that we just created in above steps and recreating as bellows:

```
DROP INDEX [IX_TblEmployee_City] ON [IMS].[dbo].[TblEmployee]
GO

CREATE NONCLUSTERED INDEX [IX_TblEmployee_City]
ON [IMS].[dbo].[TblEmployee] ([City])
WHERE ([City] IS NOT NULL)
```

In order to make sure that above index is actually used by the SQL statement, you can provide an index hint in query:

```
SELECT * FROM [IMS].[dbo].[TblEmployee]
    WITH (INDEX (IX_TblEmployee_City))
WHERE CITY IN ('Dallas', 'Houston')
```

If you check execution plan, you will notice that it is using Index Seek (NonClustered): IX_TblEmployee_City that we specified above.

## 7.8 COVERING INDEX

**COVERING INDEX**: A *covering index* is a non-clustered index that includes all the columns that are mentioned in the query and since, all the columns are existing in the index itself, optimizer does not need to do additional lookup to the table for fetching the data and therefore, this index significantly speed up the retrieval of data. For e.g., we have to fetch first name, last name and city of all employees, we will use following SQL command:

```
CREATE NONCLUSTERED INDEX [IX_TblEmployee_FirstName_LastName_City] ON
[IMS].[dbo].[TblEmployee]
(
    [FirstName], [LastName], [City]
)
```

You can also use *include* column SQL command as below to create a *covering index*:

```
DROP INDEX [IX_TblEmployee_FirstName_LastName_City]
ON [IMS].[dbo].[TblEmployee]

CREATE NONCLUSTERED INDEX [IX_TblEmployee_FirstName_LastName_City]
ON [IMS].[dbo].[TblEmployee]
(
    [FirstName], [LastName]
)
```

```
INCLUDE ([City] )
```

It is possible to disable an index, however, by doing so, will prevent the fetching of data and if you try to run a simple SELECT SQL statement, you will see a message: The query processor is unable to produce a plan because the index 'IX_TblEmployee_EmployeeID' on table or view 'TblEmployee' is disabled.

## 7.9 GENERAL INDEX GUIDELINES

### General Index Guidelines:

1. Indexing on small tables are generally avoided since it is much faster to perform table scan directly rather than SQL optimizer going to index and finding the data leaf.

2. Indexes need to be designed so that they are narrow meaning that indexes need to comprise as few columns as absolutely required.

3. Tables do not need to be over-indexed especially the ones that are frequently updated since, it will require to update the indexes as well, e.g., a batch that performs several DML operations.

Over a period of time, due to various data manipulation operations (insert, update, delete), index fragmentation occurs and hence, database performance deteriorates. So, it is important to defrag or rebuild indexes over periodic interval depending how many DML operations are taking place. In order to check index fragmentation, SQL Server provides a DMV (**D**ata **M**anagement **V**iew) to provide this info: *sys.dm_db_index_physical_stats* OR *DBCC SHOWCONTIG* can be used as well.

```
SELECT * FROM sys.dm_db_index_physical_stats(DB_ID('IMS'),
OBJECT_ID('IMS.dbo.TblEmployee'), NULL, NULL, NULL);
```

| database_id | object_id | index_id | index_type_desc | avg_fragmentation_in_percent |
|---|---|---|---|---|
| 5 | 1541580530 | 0 | HEAP | 0 |
| 5 | 1541580530 | 3 | NONCLUSTERED INDEX | 0 |

```
DBCC SHOWCONTIG ('IMS.dbo.TblEmployee')
GO
```

The result returned provides level of index

```
DBCC SHOWCONTIG scanning 'TblEmployee' table...
Table: 'TblEmployee' (1541580530); index ID: 0, database ID: 5
TABLE level scan performed.
- Pages Scanned................................: 1
- Extents Scanned..............................: 1
- Extent Switches..............................: 0
- Avg. Pages per Extent........................: 1.0
- Scan Density [Best Count:Actual Count].......: 100.00% [1:1]
```

```
- Extent Scan Fragmentation ...................: 0.00%
- Avg. Bytes Free per Page.....................: 7960.0
- Avg. Page Density (full)....................: 1.66%
DBCC execution completed. If DBCC printed error messages, contact your system administrator.
```

You can also use Database Tuning Advisor to make recommendations for indexes and incorporate them into database design. There are several other performance tools like *Redgate, Idera, Foglight*, etc., available in market to monitor the database performance.

## Chapter 8: Views: Partitioned, Encryption, Schema Binding, Indexed, and Synonyms

A *view* is like a virtual table that consists of columns from one or several tables but it is not stored in the database, only SQL query is stored and the tables are referred as *underlying base* tables. Whenever you call a *view,* it shows the latest data from the base tables. Since underlying base tables are not directly queried by the user, a view adds a security layer to the data. So, the permission can be granted to the *view* without having to provide access to tables. Also, even if the table schema is changed, user can keep using the view without any changes to the code.

### 8.1 VIEW

**VIEW**: A *view* is created by using SELECT statement. For e.g., you want to get all the customers without providing direct access to *TblCustomer* table.

a. Go to **Studio** -> Expand **IMS** node under **Databases** -> Right Click on **Views** node -> Select **New View...**

b. In **Add Table** message box, select *TblCustomer* table -> Click on **Add** button -> Press **Close**.

c. Choose FirstName, Lastname and City columns from *TblCustomer* table as shown in below Fig.

d. Click on **Save** button on toolbar and enter the name of view as **vwCustomer.**

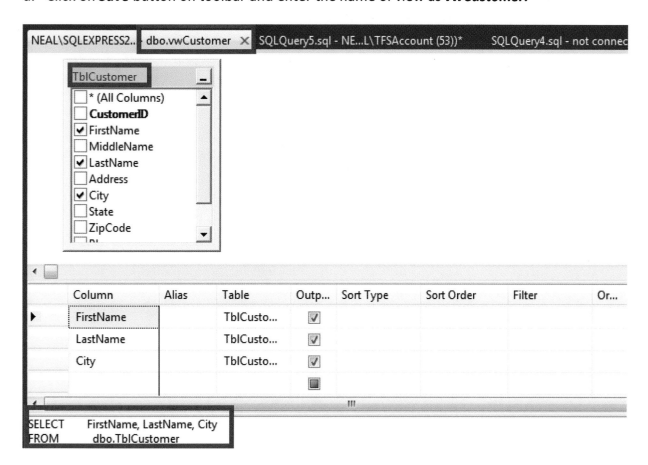

Following SQL command can be run to fetch the customer data using the above created view **vwCustomer**, not from *TblCustomer* table.

```
SELECT TOP 1000
    [FirstName]
    ,[LastName]
    ,[City]
FROM [IMS].[dbo].[vwCustomer]
```

Instead of using Management Studio, you could also run following SQL command to create the same view:

```
USE IMS
GO

CREATE VIEW [dbo].[vwCustomer]
AS
SELECT
    FirstName, LastName, City
FROM
    dbo.TblCustomer
GO
```

Note that view can only be created on current database and therefore, you can not specify name of database in **CREATE VIEW [IMS].dbo.[vwCustomer]**. If you do so, it will give an error message: CREATE/ALTER VIEW does not allow specifying the database name as a prefix to the object name. You can also specify any WHERE clause in SQL command or even grouping if required.

If you want to change the definition of view later on, there is no need to drop it and re-create it. You can always update a *view* by following SQL command:

```
--Modify an existing view
ALTER VIEW [dbo].[vwCustomer]
AS
SELECT
    FirstName, LastName, City
FROM
    dbo.TblCustomer
GO
```

In case you want to get info about just created view, you can use following SQL command:

```
USE IMS
GO
SELECT definition, is_schema_bound
FROM sys.sql_modules
WHERE object_id = OBJECT_ID('vwCustomer')
```

```
GO
EXEC sp_helptext 'vwCustomer'
```

Note that you can perform the DML (insert, update, delete) operations using the views under certain scenarios: if the view does not use joins, aggregates or group by clauses.

## 8.2 ENCRYPTION VIEW

**ENCRYPTION VIEW**: This is just like a regular view except that that the definition of the view cannot be seen by users and therefore, it makes it secure from hacking. Also, it prevents view from publication in SQL Server replication.

```
USE IMS
GO

DROP VIEW [dbo].[vwCustomer]
GO

CREATE VIEW vwCustomer
WITH ENCRYPTION
AS
SELECT
    FirstName, LastName, City
FROM
    IMS.dbo.TblCustomer
GO
```

After executing above SQL commands, you will see *vwCustomer* view listed under **Views** node and if you do not see, right click and press **Refresh**. Note that a yellow lock icon with this view, indicating that it is an encrypted view. Notice that if you right click on *vwCustomer* view, **design** option is greyed out. Also, if try to script view definition: right click on *vwCustomer -> Script View as -> CREATE to -> New Query Editor Window,* an error message will be displayed.

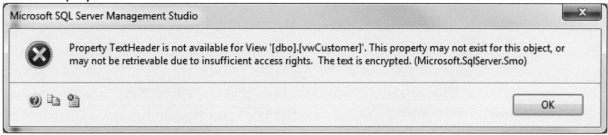

Note that once a view has been encrypted, it cannot be decrypted and would need to be modified or recreated.

## 8.3 PARTITIONED VIEW

**PARTITIONED VIEW**: This type of view combine results of several selects from multiple tables into a single result by using UNION operator. For e.g., if you have 2 partitions existing on 2 servers and you can create a *partitioned view* as follows:

```
CREATE VIEW vwGetInfoServers
AS
    -- Server1 has TblPartitionTable1 data
    SELECT *
     FROM [IMS].[dbo].[TblPartitionTable1]
UNION ALL
    -- Server 2 has TblPartitionTable2 data
    SELECT *
     FROM [Server2].[IMS].[dbo].[TblPartitionTable2]
```

## 8.4 SYSTEM VIEW

**SYSTEM VIEW**: This type of view exposes the database metadata and can be used to get info about the SQL server instance or the objects residing in that instance. For e.g., if you need to get names of all the databases existing in an instance:

```
SELECT * FROM sys.databases -- System View
```

## 8.5 SCHEMABINDING VIEW

**SCHEMABINDING VIEW**: *Schemabinding* ties the view to the underlying base table or table's schema, meaning that schema of base table or tables cannot be changed that would impact the view definition. If the table schema needs to be modified, view needs to be either dropped or modified first to exclude dependencies.

```
CREATE VIEW vwGetInfoCustomer
WITH SCHEMABINDING
AS
SELECT
    FirstName, LastName, Address, City, State, ZipCode
FROM
    dbo.TblCustomer
GO
```
*Schemabinding* provides a protection to the view that table definition cannot be changed, unless view is modified first.

## 8.6 INDEXED VIEW

**INDEXED VIEW**: A view that has an index associated with it is known as *indexed view*. The first index created on a view has to be a unique clustered index and then non-clustered indexes can be created. This improves the performance of query due to the same reason that index (clustered) is stored on the disk.

```
USE [IMS]
GO


--Drop existing view to create indexed view
DROP VIEW [dbo].[vwCustomer]
GO


-- Create a view
CREATE VIEW [dbo].[vwCustomer]
WITH SCHEMABINDING
AS
SELECT
    FirstName, LastName, City
FROM
    [dbo].[TblCustomer]
GO


--Create an index on the view.
CREATE UNIQUE CLUSTERED INDEX IX_vwCustomer
ON vwCustomer (FirstName)
```

It needs to be noted that if the underlying table undergoes frequent changes, then, having indexed view may not be optimal for query performance.

## 8.7 WITH CHECK VIEW

**WITH CHECK VIEW**: Views can be used to perform DML (insert, update, delete) operations, however, if we want to make sure that these DML operation take place under certain conditions, for e.g., update the first name of customer if they belong to Houston city, you can create a view *WITH CHECK* as below:

```
CREATE VIEW vwCustomerCheckCity
AS
SELECT
    FirstName, LastName, City
FROM
    [dbo].[TblCustomer]
WHERE City = 'Houston'
WITH CHECK OPTION
GO
```
This check imposes any changes to the *TblCustomer* data only if the city is Houston.

## 8.8 SYNONYMS

**Synonyms:** A synonym is an alternative name for database objects like tables, views, stored procedures, functions, etc. and provides a layer of abstraction over the database object, helping in protecting the change in name of object or the location of the object. For e.g., if you have a three-part name of the table: *DatabaseName.SchemaName.TableName: IMS.dbo.TblCustomer* and say we assign a synonym (**syCustomer**) to this table, and if you use *syCustomer* in your application and later on table name changes to something else, your application code will remain unchanged and therefore, there is no need to be re-deploy to production environment.

```
--Create a synonym for TblCustomer table
CREATE SYNONYM syCustomer
FOR [IMS].[dbo].[TblCustomer];
GO
-- Check existing synonyms
USE MASTER
GO
SELECT * FROM sys.synonyms
GO
```

In next Chapter 9, we will look at various types of stored procedures.

## Chapter 9: Stored Procedures:  User-Defined, I/P, O/P, Encryption, System, Extended, Temporary

*Stored procedure (SP)* is a collection of several T-SQL statements grouped together to achieve a desired query result. These bunch of statements are compiled inside SQL Server and stored as such, provides a much faster execution as a result of compiled code as compared to individual T-SQL statements, and are safer from hacking attempts, so called **SQL-injection** where hackers try to query databases by brute trial-and-error attempts in order to steal data. Since T-SQL statements are packaged into a stored procedure, they can be re-used multiple times in multiple applications and by multiple users and hence, helps achieve code re-usability, modularity and leading to better database architectural designs, and as a result, code maintenance is improved as well. These advantages of stored procedure are summarized as below:

a. *Code Re-usability*
b. *Performance Enhancement*
c. *Safer Code and Higher Security*
d. *Maintenance Improvement*
e. *Lesser Network Load* (since T-SQL statements are stored on SQL Server and they are not passed in each and every request to server)

Due to above reasons, understanding stored procedure is important and its proper implementation is critical to improving performance of overall database design. We will discuss about different types of SPs as below.

## 9.1 USER-DEFINED STORED PROCEDURE

A user-defined SP (USP) is created as following:

a. Go to **Studio** -> Expand **IMS** node under **Databases** (click on + sign) -> Expand **Programmability** node -> Expand **Stored Procedures** node -> Right Click on **Stored Procedures** node -> Select **New Stored Procedure...** You will be displayed a new SP in Query Editor Window.
b. Enter the *Author* name, *Create date* and *Description* of SP: e.g., get list of customers.
c. Change the name of SP appropriately what this SP will perform: **uspIMSGetCustomers.** Note that we are prefixing **usp** to the name of SP, to indicate that it is a **u**ser-defined **s**tored **p**rocedure and also database name: **IMS** to easily identify where a stored procedure belongs to, which are again part of naming convention and each company can have their standards.
d. Remove both the parameters: Param1 and Param2 since we are not passing any input parameters in this example.
e. Enter the SQL statements to fetch the customers and SP will look as below.

```
USE IMS
GO
-- =============================================
-- Author:      Neal Gupta
```

```
-- Create date: 09/01/2013
-- Description: Get list of customers
-- =================================================
CREATE PROCEDURE uspIMSGetCustomers
AS
BEGIN
    -- SET NOCOUNT ON added to prevent extra result sets from
    -- interfering with SELECT statements.
    SET NOCOUNT ON;

    SELECT
            [CustomerID]
           ,[FirstName]
           ,[MiddleName]
           ,[LastName]
           ,[Address]
           ,[City]
           ,[State]
           ,[ZipCode]
           ,[Phone]
           ,[Country]
    FROM [dbo].[TblCustomer]
END
```

f.  Press **Execute** OR simply press F5 to create this stored procedure. If everything is ok, you
    will see a message: *Command(s) completed successfully*.

g.  Right click on **Stored Procedures** node -> Refresh and you will see above stored
    procedure listed there as below.

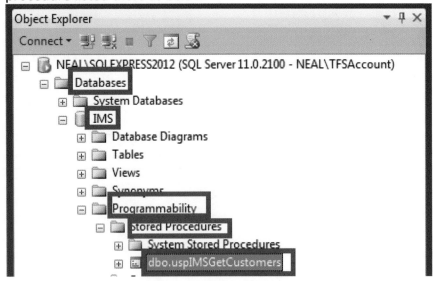

h.  Now that you have created a new stored procedure, you can run it in following 2 ways:
    1.  Right Click on SP: ***uspIMSGetCustomers*** -> Select ***Execute Stored Procedure..*** ->
        Press OK and you will see the list of customers returned. OR
    2.  Use the SQL commands as below:

```
    EXEC [dbo].[uspIMSGetCustomers]
```

## 9.2 INPUT PARAMETER SP

A stored procedure can be created that accepts one or more than one input parameters, .e.g., you want to get list of all orders for a given *CustomerID*, which is considered as an input parameter.

1. *Single Input Parameter SP*: This stored procedure will be passed with a single input parameter:

```
USE IMS
GO
-- ================================================
-- Description: Get list of customers
-- ================================================
CREATE PROCEDURE uspIMSGetOrdersByCustomerID
      @CustomerID INT -- SINGLE INPUT PARAMETER
AS
BEGIN
      SET NOCOUNT ON;

      -- Get orders for an input CustomerID
      SELECT
            [OrderID]
           ,[CustomerID]
           ,[ProductID]
           ,[OrderQty]
           ,[OrderDate]
           ,[IsOrderActive]
           ,[Comment]
      FROM [IMS].[dbo].[TblOrder]
      WHERE CustomerID = @CustomerID
END
```

Once you execute above SP, it will ask for 1 input parameter and enter 1 as *customerID:*
```
EXEC [dbo].[uspIMSGetOrdersByCustomerID] @CustomerID = 1
```

2. *Multiple Input Parameters SP*: A stored procedure where you pass more than a single input parameter is considered as multiple input parameters SP, e.g., fetch all the products ordered for *OrderID* = 1 for *CustomerID* = 1:

```
USE IMS
GO
-- ================================================
-- Description: Get Products for OrderID/CustomerID
-- ================================================
CREATE PROCEDURE uspIMSGetProductsByOrderIDAndCustomerID
      @OrderID INT
     ,@CustomerID INT
AS
BEGIN
```

```
    SET NOCOUNT ON;

    -- Get products ordered for a given OrderID and CustomerID
    SELECT
            [ProductID]
           ,[OrderQty]
           ,[OrderDate]
           ,[IsOrderActive]
           ,[Comment]
    FROM [IMS].[dbo].[TblOrder]
    WHERE OrderID = @OrderID
        AND CustomerID = @CustomerID
END
```

First execute the above SQL commands to create stored procedure and run it as below:

```
EXEC [dbo].[uspIMSGetProductsByOrderIDAndCustomerID]
     @OrderID = 1
    ,@CustomerID = 1
```

Input parameters can be made *optional*, meaning that, those parameters are not required to be passed to the stored procedure. In order to do, you will declare input parameters as NULL as below, meaning that it is not necessary to pass those input parameters; otherwise, if you do not pass all the required input parameters, SQL Server will raise an error.

```
CREATE PROCEDURE uspIMSGetTestData
        @Param1 INT NULL
```

## 9.3 OUTPUT PARAMETER SP

This stored procedure can contain a single or multiple output parameters, which is just opposite of *input parameter SP*, where instead of passing input parameters, rather output parameters are returned by the stored procedure. For e.g., if we want to get the maximum price of all the products, it can be returned as output parameter as below:

```
USE IMS
GO
-- ================================================
-- Description: Get Maximum price of all products
-- ================================================
CREATE PROCEDURE uspIMSGetMaxPriceProducts
    @MaxPrice INT OUTPUT -- OUTPUT PARAMETER
AS
BEGIN
    SET NOCOUNT ON;

    SELECT @MaxPrice = MAX(Price)
    FROM [IMS].[dbo].[TblProduct]
END
```

Above stored procedure can be run as below:

```
DECLARE  @MaxPrice INT
```

```
EXEC [dbo].[uspIMSGetMaxPriceProducts] @MaxPrice = @MaxPrice OUTPUT
SELECT    @MaxPrice AS '@MaxPrice'
```

## 9.4 INPUT OUTPUT PARAMETERS SP

This stored procedure contains both input and output parameters, each of which can be a single and multiple parameters. For e.g., we want to fetch the invoice total for a given customer as below:

```
USE IMS
GO
-- ================================================
-- Description: Get Invoice total for a Customer
-- ================================================
CREATE PROCEDURE uspIMSGetInvoiceTotalByCustomerID
    @CustomerID INT    -- INPUT PARAMETER
    ,@InvoiceTotal DECIMAL(9,2) OUTPUT -- OUTPUT PARAMETER
AS
BEGIN
   SELECT @InvoiceTotal = SUM(O.OrderQty * P.Price)
      FROM [IMS].[dbo].[TblOrder] O
   INNER JOIN [IMS].[dbo].[TblProduct] P
      ON P.ProductID = O.ProductID
   WHERE CustomerID = @CustomerID
END
```

Above stored procedure is executed for a *CustomerID* and invoice total is returned as output parameter as below:

```
DECLARE  @InvoiceTotal decimal(9, 2)

EXEC     @return_value = [dbo].[uspIMSGetInvoiceTotalByCustomerID]
         @CustomerID = 1,
         @InvoiceTotal = @InvoiceTotal OUTPUT

SELECT   @InvoiceTotal as '@InvoiceTotal'
```

## 9.5 ENCRYPTION SP

**ENCRYPTION SP**: Just like, a view can be encrypted so that the definition is hidden, similarly, we can create a stored procedure with encryption that will hide its definition, though, it is not frequently done, however, if situation demands and there is any sensitive contents inside a SP, we can do so:

```
USE IMS
GO
CREATE PROCEDURE uspIMSGetProducts
WITH ENCRYPTION
AS
BEGIN
   SET NOCOUNT ON;
```

```
SELECT
        [ProductID]
        ,[Name]
        ,[Description]
        ,[Manufacturer]
        ,[QtyAvailable]
        ,[Price]
    FROM [IMS].[dbo].[TblProduct]
END
GO
```

Notice that a lock icon is displayed along with the stored procedure name and if right click on this stored procedure inside Studio's object explorer, *modify* option will be greyed out.

Note that once you have encrypted a SP, you will not be able to view its contents in future and therefore, it is important to keep a backup copy of encrypted stored procedure in safe place like source control: **P**olytron **V**ersion **C**ontrol **S**ystem (PVCS), **V**isual **S**ource **S**afe (VSS), **T**eam **F**oundation **S**erver (TFS) 2010 or TFS 2012, see author's book on TFS for more details.

## 9.6 SYSTEM SP (SSP)

System stored procedures are generated by SQL Server during the creation of new database and support various administrative and informational tasks. There are many categories of system SP and few are mentioned below:

a. **Catalog SSP**: *sp_columns, sp_tables, sp_statistics, sp_server_info, sp_pkeys, sp_stored_procedures*

b. Database Engine SSP: *sp_help, sp_helptext, sp_helpfile, sp_who, sp_execute, sp_helpindex*

c. Cursor SSP

d. Log Shipping SSP

e. Full-Text Search SSP, etc.

For example, if we want to see definition of any of the stored procedure that we created, system stored procedure (SSP) can help you in getting this info as below:

```
-- Using a System SP (SSP)
EXEC sp_helptext uspIMSGetCustomers
```

However, as we mentioned in #5, if you try to see definition of encrypted stored procedure, you will see message displayed as below, since definition is hidden:

```
EXEC sp_helptext uspIMSGetProducts
```

```
The text for object 'uspIMSGetProducts' is encrypted.
```

Also, notice that system stored procedure have a prefix of **sp_** and therefore, we should not name any of user-defined stored procedure with this prefix. Note that you can also create a system stored procedure by naming it with **sp_** prefix and placing it in **master** database.

## 9.7 EXTENDED SP (ESP)

Extended stored procedures are used to provide an interface or connection to external applications for custom maintenance tasks. Below are some system stored procedures that help achieve extension of such tasks:

a. *xp_sprintf*
b. *xp_logevent*
c. *xp_grantlogin, etc.*

For e.g., below SP can support logging message to the windows OS's *event viewer*:

```
USE master
EXEC xp_logevent 10000, 'Test', informational
```

## 9.8 EXTENDED USER-DEFINED SP (EUSP) / CLR SP

Extended user-defined stored procedures support creating external functions that can be written in various programming language like C or C# that can leverage full power of .NET framework 3.5 or 4.5. Now, these EUSP have been overtaken by **C**ommon **L**anguage **R**untime (CLR) procedures that provide high flexibility in developing custom features and can be called inside other user-defined procedures. For e.g., if you have encryption keys that you want to hide and not show to anyone else, you can put those in CLR procedures. These CLR procedures are compiled into a **D**ynamic **L**inked **L**ibrary (DLL) file and loaded into SQL Server.

You can view extended stored procedures as below:

```
SELECT * FROM master.sys.extended_procedures
```

## 9.9 TEMPORARY SP

As name suggests, these stored procedures are stored temporarily in *tempdb* database: there are 2 flavors: *private temporary SP* and *global temporary SP* and are created using # and ## respectively. Once the SQL server is shutdown, these stored procedures no longer exist.

In the next Chapter 10, we will look at various *functions*, which have some of the similar features as stored procedures; however, there are circumstances where one may be suitable or other.

## Chapter 10: Functions: UDFs, SVF, ITVF, MSTVF, Aggregate, System, CLR

A *U*ser-*D*efined *F*unction (UDF) is similar to stored procedure, that we saw in previous Chapter 9, that takes a single or multiple input values and perform some computations, except that it always return a value of a defined typed, which can be *scalar* (single) value or a *table*. Since there is a return value, it is used inside an expression, and unlike stored procedure, it is not invoked with an *execute* statement. A function can call another function and nesting can be up to 32 levels and is invoked along with schema name e.g., *dbo*. Name of a function can be up to 128 characters. Inside a function, a DML operation (*insert, update, delete*) cannot be performed unlike stored procedure. These features of UDFs are summarized as below:

a. *Can do nesting of functions.*
b. *Cannot call stored procedures, but can call extended SPs.*
c. *No modification of database tables allowed.*
d. *Can take input parameters*
e. *Cannot contains output parameters*
f. *Cannot use error handling: try-catch*

Different types of user-defined functions are explained as below.

## 10.1 SCALAR-VALUED FUNCTION (SVF)

A scalar-valued function (SVF) is created as follows:

a. Go to **Studio** -> Expand **IMS** node under **Databases** (click on + sign) -> Expand **Programmability** node -> Expand **Functions** node -> Right Click on **Scalar-valued Functions** node -> Select **New Scalar-valued Function...** You will be displayed a new UDF template in Query Editor Window.

b. Enter the *Author* name, *Create date* and *Description* of UDF: e.g., get total of customers.

c. Change the name of UDF appropriately what it will do: **svfIMSGetTotCustomers.** Note that we are prefixing **svf** to the name of UDF, to indicate that it is **s**calar-**v**alued **f**unction and also database name: **IMS** to easily identify where a function belongs to, which are again part of naming convention and each company can have their standards.

d. Remove both the parameters: Param1 and Param2 since we are not passing any input parameters in this example.

e. Enter the SQL statements to get the total of customers and UDF will look as below.

```
USE IMS
GO

-- =============================================
-- Author:       Neal Gupta
-- Create date: 10/01/2013
-- Description: Get total of customers
-- =============================================
CREATE FUNCTION [dbo].[svfIMSGetTotCustomers]
(
)
RETURNS INT
AS
```

```
BEGIN
        -- Declare the return variable here
        DECLARE @TotCustomers INT

        SELECT @TotCustomers = COUNT(CustomerID)
        FROM [IMS].[dbo].[TblCustomer]

        -- Return the result of the function
        RETURN @TotCustomers
END
```

You can use following SQL statement to invoke the above user-defined function:

```
SELECT [dbo].[svfIMSGetTotCustomers]()
```

Notice that we did not pass any input value (empty parenthesis) to above UDF. However, in below example, we will pass a single input value.

```
USE IMS
GO
-- ================================================
-- Description: Get Qty of product available
-- ================================================
CREATE FUNCTION [dbo].[svfIMSGetQtyProduct]
(
        @ProductID INT
)
RETURNS INT
AS
BEGIN
        DECLARE @QtyAvailable INT

        SELECT @QtyAvailable = QtyAvailable
        FROM [IMS].[dbo].[TblProduct]
        WHERE ProductID = @ProductID

        -- Return the result of the function
        RETURN @QtyAvailable
END
```

The above scalar UDF can be called using following SQL statement:

```
SELECT ProductID, [dbo].[svfIMSGetQtyProduct](ProductID)
FROM [IMS].[dbo].[TblProduct]
```

## 10.2 INLINE TABLE-VALUED FUNCTION (I-TVF)

This is a UDF that returns a data type of *table*, a set of rows, and is similar to set of data returned by *view*, however, TVF provides much more capability than view, which are limited to one *select* SQL statement. TVF can have logic and multiple statements from one or more tables. TVF can replace a stored procedure and TVF are invoked using the *select,* unlike stored procedure that needs to be executed. For example, we want to get all the orders for the products, a inline TVF is created below:

```
USE IMS
GO
-- ================================================
-- Description: Get orders for products
-- ================================================
CREATE FUNCTION [dbo].[tvfIMSGetProductOrders]
(
)
RETURNS TABLE
AS
RETURN
(
    SELECT [OrderID], [CustomerID], [ProductID], [OrderQty],
           [OrderDate], [Comment]
    FROM [IMS].[dbo].[TblOrder]
)
```

You can run following SQL statement to call above inline TVF:
```
SELECT * FROM [dbo].[tvfIMSGetProductOrders]()
```

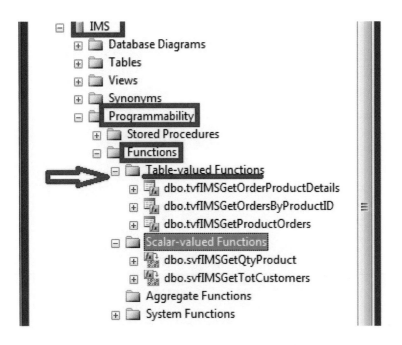

Note that in above inline TVF, input parameter was not passed. However, if we want to get all the orders for a product ID, we can use following inline TVF:

```
USE IMS
GO
-- ================================================
-- Description: Get orders for a product
-- ================================================
```

```sql
CREATE FUNCTION  [dbo].[tvfIMSGetOrdersByProductID]
(
    @ProductID INT
)
RETURNS TABLE
AS
RETURN
(
    SELECT [OrderID], [CustomerID], [ProductID], [OrderQty],
          [OrderDate], [Comment]
    FROM [IMS].[dbo].[TblOrder]
    WHERE ProductID = @ProductID
)
```

Similarly, you can invoke above inline TVF as follows:
```sql
SELECT * FROM [dbo].[tvfIMSGetOrdersByProductID](2)
```

## 10.3 MULTI-STATEMENT TABLE-VALUED FUNCTION (MS-TVF)

Similar to *inline TVF* as explained above, multi-statement TVF returns a *table*, however, the returned table needs to be defined first, rows are inserted to this table, and returned to the caller. For e.g., if we want to get the order details of a product, we will create a *multi-statement TVF* as below:

```sql
USE IMS
GO
-- ================================================
-- Description: Get order details for a product
-- ================================================
CREATE FUNCTION  [dbo].[tvfIMSGetOrderProductDetails]
(
    @ProductID INT
)
RETURNS @OrderProductDetails TABLE
(
     OrderID INT NOT NULL
    ,OrderDate DATETIME
    ,ProductID INT
    ,Name VARCHAR(50)
    ,Price DECIMAL(9,2)
)
AS
BEGIN
    INSERT INTO @OrderProductDetails
    SELECT
          O.OrderID, O.OrderDate
         ,P.ProductID, P.Name, P.Price
    FROM [IMS].[dbo].[TblOrder] O
    INNER JOIN [IMS].[dbo].[TblProduct] P
          ON O.ProductID = P.ProductID
```

```
    WHERE O.ProductID =  @ProductID

    -- Return the row data in above table
    RETURN
END
```

Above multi-statement TVF is invoked using following SQL statement:
```
SELECT * FROM [dbo].[tvfIMSGetOrderProductDetails](5)
```

## 10.4 AGGREGATE FUNCTION

These functions give you summarized info like average of salary, total count of products, minimum and maximum, etc. Aggregate functions are actually part of *system functions* (mentioned next) and some of these are mentioned as below:

a. **COUNT**(): Counts all the rows: *Count*(*), *Count*(ALL Column), *Count*(*DISTINCT* Column): Counts only distinct rows.
b. **AVG**(): Average value of the column used
c. **SUM**(): Totals of values for column provided
d. **MAX**(), **MIN**(): Max or Min value of the value for column
e. **STDEV**(): Get the standard deviation value for column

## 10.5 SYSTEM FUNCTION

These are in-built functions inside the SQL Server and helps in executing various operations related to date time (*GETDATE, GETUTCDATE, DATE, MONTH, YEAR, DATEADD, DATEPART, ISDATE*), security (*USER, USER_ID, USER_NAME, IS_MEMBER*), string manipulation (*CHARINDEX, RTRIM, LTRIM, SUBSTRING, LOWER, UPPER, LEN*), mathematical (*ABS, COS, SIN, SQUARE, PI*), etc. as shown in below Fig. We will see some of these functions used in later chapters.

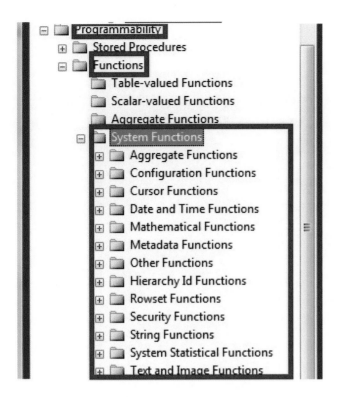

## 10.6 CLR FUNCTION

Common Language Runtime (CLR) function is created inside a DLL, similar to CLR stored procedure that we discussed in last chapter and normally reserved for customized tasks.

Similar to stored procedure, you can create *schemabinding UDF* or *encryption scalar or table-valued UDF* using following options:

## 10.7 SCHEMABINDING AND ENCRYPTION UDF

A. **SCHEMABINDING UDF**: Once UDF is schema bind, underlying database table cannot be deleted:

```
CREATE FUNCTION [dbo].[svfIMSSchemaFn]
(
)
RETURNS INT
WITH SCHEMABINDING
AS
BEGIN
  ...
END
```

B. **ENCRYPTION UDF**: Once an encrypted UDF is created, definition is hidden and cannot be viewed later.

```
CREATE FUNCTION [dbo].[svfIMSEncryptionFn]
(
) RETURNS DECIMAL(9,2)
WITH ENCRYPTION
```

```
BEGIN
  . . .
END
```

If you want to modify an existing function, *ALTER FUNCTION* is used which keeps underlying security privileges for the UDF intact. For deleting a UDF, *DROP FUNCTION* is used.

In next Chapter 11, we will learn about *triggers* that can help in performing additional data manipulation tasks on the tables, while doing DML tasks.

## Chapter 11: Triggers: DML, DDL, After, Instead Of, DB, Server, Logon

Trigger is a special type of stored procedure that is executed, invoked or *fired*, automatically, when a certain database event occurs like DML (*insert, update, delete*) operation. However, trigger cannot be passed any value and does not return a value. A trigger is fired either *before* or *after* a database event and associated with a *table* or a *view*. Trigger can also be used to check the integrity of data before or after an event occurs and can rollback a transaction. There are 3 categorizes of triggers:

a. *DML Triggers*: Fire on DML operations (insert, update, delete)
b. *DDL Triggers*: Fire on DDL operations (*create, alter, drop, grant*)
c. *Logon Triggers*: Fire in response to *LOGON* event.

Multiple triggers can also be created on the same table or view, even for the same database event. Also, triggers can be nested, meaning if the trigger changes another table on which there is another trigger, and so on, and there can be up to 32 levels of nesting. Triggers should be used when absolutely required due to potential for extra I/O overhead; otherwise, stored procedures or functions need to be considered.

We will go over different types of triggers as below:

## 11.1 DML Triggers (DML-TR)

**11.1.1 AFTER TRIGGER**: This *AFTER trigger* is fired whenever a DML statement as specified in trigger occurs, as below. Note that *FOR trigger* is same as AFTER trigger.

```
USE IMS
GO

IF OBJECT_ID ('trgIMSTblCustomerInsertUpdate', 'TR') IS NOT NULL
  DROP TRIGGER trgIMSTblCustomerInsertUpdate


-- ================================================
-- Author:      Neal Gupta
-- Create date: 11/01/2013
-- Description: Create a trigger for Insert, Update
-- ================================================
CREATE TRIGGER trgIMSTblCustomerInsertUpdate
    ON [IMS].[dbo].[TblCustomer]
    AFTER INSERT, UPDATE
AS
BEGIN
    SET NOCOUNT ON;

    -- SQL statements for trigger here
    PRINT 'trgIMSTblCustomerInsertUpdate Invoked'

    -- Add any other SQL statement
```

END

Now, if you run below Insert SQL statement, above trigger is fired:

```
INSERT INTO [IMS].[dbo].[TblCustomer] ([FirstName],[MiddleName],
[LastName],[Address],[City],[State],[ZipCode],[Phone],[Country])
VALUES ('John', '', 'Doe', '123 Denton Rd', 'Seattle', 'WA', '10006',
'623-456-7890', 'USA')
```

You will notice that in **Messages** Tab in Studio, below message is printed, indicating that trigger: *trgIMSTblCustomerInsert* is called after the *insert* is performed.

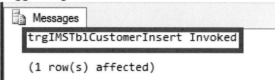

Note that when an *insert* or *update* SQL statement runs, a copy of new row is added into *INSERTED* table and can be accessed within a trigger to perform additional checks or rollback a transaction, if there is some violation of data integrity. Similarly, when a *delete* SQL statement runs, a copy of deleted rows is added to *DELETED* table.

Above triggers are also classified as follows:
1. **After Insert Trigger**: AFTER Trigger for *insert* SQL statement
2. **After Update Trigger**: AFTER Trigger for *update* SQL statement
3. **After Delete Trigger**: AFTER Trigger for *delete* SQL statement, as below.

Note that you can have a trigger on any combination of *insert* or *update* or *delete* or *all* of these DML operations in one trigger.

```
USE IMS
GO
-- ================================================
-- Description: Create a trigger for delete
-- ================================================
CREATE TRIGGER trgIMSTblCustomerDelete
    ON [IMS].[dbo].[TblCustomer]
    AFTER DELETE
AS
IF EXISTS (SELECT * FROM DELETED)
BEGIN
    SET NOCOUNT ON;
    DECLARE @CountDeleted INT
    SET @CountDeleted = (SELECT COUNT(*) FROM DELETED)

    PRINT 'trgIMSTblCustomerDelete Invoked'
    PRINT CAST(@CountDeleted AS VARCHAR(5)) + ' rows deleted from
    TblCustomer table'
END
```

In order for SQL server to fire above delete trigger, run following delete SQL statement:

```
DELETE FROM [IMS].[dbo].[TblCustomer]
WHERE CustomerID = 6
```

You will see below message, indicating that above delete trigger: *trgIMSTblCustomer Delete* was fired:

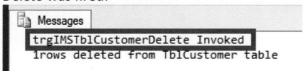

***11.1.2 INSTEAD OF TRIGGER***: When *INSTEAD OF trigger* is activated or fired on a DML operation, alternative action as defined inside a trigger takes place, meaning, for e.g., if you run an *insert* SQL statement to add a new row, that row will not be really added, unless, *Instead Of* trigger dictate to add that new row. Similar to AFTER triggers, these triggers are also categorized into 3 types:

1. ***INSTEAD OF Insert Trigger***:  INSTEAD OF Trigger fired for *insert* SQL statement
2. ***INSTEAD OF Update Trigger***:  INSTEAD OF Trigger fired for *update* SQL statement
3. ***INSTEAD OF delete Trigger***:  INSTEAD OF Trigger fired for *delete* SQL statement

```
USE IMS
GO
INSERT INTO [IMS].[dbo].[TblProduct]
([Name],[Description],[Manufacturer],[QtyAvailable],[Price])
VALUES ('UHDTV', 'Ultra-Hi Smart 3D TV', 'LG', 1, 50000.00)


-- =================================================
-- Description: Create INSTEAD OF trigger for delete
-- =================================================
CREATE TRIGGER trgIMSTblProductInsteadOfDelete
   ON [IMS].[dbo].[TblProduct]
   INSTEAD OF DELETE
AS
BEGIN
     SET NOCOUNT ON;

     DECLARE @ProductID INT
     SELECT @ProductID = (SELECT ProductID FROM DELETED)

     IF (@ProductID > 0)
          BEGIN
                DELETE FROM [IMS].[dbo].[TblProduct]
                WHERE ProductID = @ProductID
          END
     ELSE
          BEGIN
                PRINT 'Error: ' + @@Error
```

```
                    END

                        PRINT 'INSTEAD OF TRIGGER Invoked:
                        trgIMSTblProductInsteadOfDelete'
                        PRINT CAST(@ProductID AS VARCHAR(5)) + ' ProductID deleted
                        from TblProduct table'
        END
        GO

        -- Run Delete SQL Query to fire above INSTEAD OF trigger
        DELETE FROM [IMS].[dbo].[TblProduct]
        WHERE Name = 'UHDTV'
```

Once you run above delete SQL statement, you will see following message in **Messages** Tab in Studio.

```
Messages
INSTEAD OF TRIGGER Invoked: trgIMSTblProductInsteadOfDelete
1008 ProductID deleted from TblProduct table
```

Note that *truncate* SQL statement does not trigger *delete* trigger, since, it does not perform individual row deletions.

## 11.2 DDL Triggers (DDL-TR)

These triggers are fired **after** a DDL statement is executed on a database, for e.g., *CREATE, ALTER, DROP, GRANT, REVOKE*, or a server related event. Some of the features of DDL triggers are summarized below:
a.  *No INSTEAD OF triggers exist*
b.  *Fire only after DDL SQL statements.*
c.  *INSERTED and DELETED tables are not created.*

Now, we will review different types of DDL triggers as below:
A.  ***DATABASE-SCOPED DDL TRIGGER (DS-DDL-TR)***:

```
USE IMS
GO
-- =============================================
-- Description: Create DDL Trigger (DS-DDL-TR)
-- =============================================
CREATE TRIGGER trgIMSDatabaseTrigger1
    ON DATABASE
    FOR ALTER_TABLE, DROP_TABLE
AS
BEGIN
        PRINT 'DLL TRIGGER Fired: ' + 'trgIMSDatabaseTrigger1'
        -- Perform a SQL operation:
        ROLLBACK
END
```

Above DDL trigger is fired once you run any alter table or drop table command. This trigger exists in Object Explorer: **Instance -> Databases -> IMS -> Programmability -> Database Triggers**, as in below Fig.

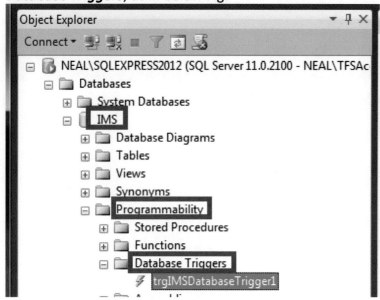

B. **SERVER-SCOPED DDL TRIGGER: (SS-DDL-TR)**: These triggers are fired when there is an event occurring at server instance, for e.g., when a database is created as below.

```
-- ================================================
-- Description:    Create DDL Trigger (SS-DDL-TR)
-- ================================================
CREATE TRIGGER trgIMSServerTrigger1
    ON ALL SERVER
    FOR CREATE_DATABASE
AS
BEGIN
        PRINT 'SERVER DLL TRIGGER Fired: ' + 'trgIMSServerTrigger1'
END
```

Once you run *create database* SQL statement, above trigger is going to fire. These server triggers are located in Object Explorer: **SQL Server Instance -> Server Objects -> Triggers,** as in below Fig.

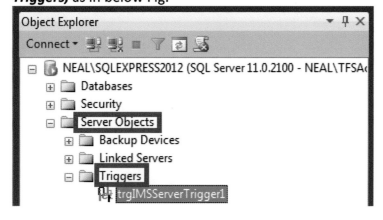

C. **CLR DLL Triggers**: These triggers are defined in an outside routine using some programming language like C#.NET and compiled into a DLL file. This DLL or *assembly* file is registered inside SQL Server. These are typically used for some specialized purpose.

## 11.3 LOGON TRIGGERS (LOG-TR)

These triggers fire when LOGON event occurs, after the authentication of logging to SQL Server instance completes. Logon trigger does not activate if the authentication of a user session fails.

```
-- ================================================
-- Description: Create LOGON Trigger
-- ================================================
CREATE TRIGGER trgSQLInstanceLogon
    ON ALL SERVER
    FOR LOGON
AS
BEGIN
    PRINT 'LOGON TRIGGER Fired: ' + 'trgSQLInstanceLogon'
    DECLARE @CountSessions INT
    SET @CountSessions = (SELECT COUNT(*) FROM sys.dm_exec_sessions
        WHERE is_user_process = 1)
    PRINT 'Count Sessions: ' + CAST(@CountSessions AS VARCHAR(5))
END
```

If you login to SQL Server instance, above *logon trigger* is fired and message is displayed in **SQL Server Logs** under **Management**, as below:

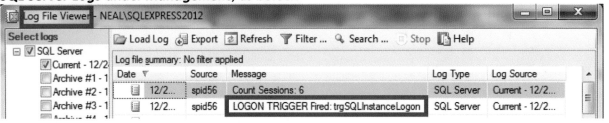

*Logon Trigger* can be used for auditing and tracking purpose or even restricting access to certain login or sessions counts.

## 11.4 MULTIPLE TRIGGERS (MUL-TR)

In case a trigger is fired when an *insert, update or delete* DML operation on a table occurs and that table already has another trigger, causing another trigger to be fired. Multiple triggers can be fired on DML, DDL or even LOGON database events.

There are two other types of triggers like *recursive* and *nested*, which allow for maximum 32 levels, however, there are only rare circumstances where these will be required.

In next Chapter 12, we will talk about *Cursors* that are sometimes used by SQL developers, though, not recommended, and as such alternative approaches are preferred.

## Chapter 12: Cursors:  Read Only, Forward Only, Fast Forward, Static, Scroll, Dynamic, Optimistic

Cursors are database objects that are used to iterate over a set of rows and generally perform some additional logical operations or others on each row of fetched data. The process of cursor operation entails following tasks:

a. *Declare the variables to be used*
b. *Define the Cursor and type of cursor*
c. *Populate Cursor with values using SELECT*
d. *Open Cursor that was declared & populated above*
e. *Fetch the values from Cursor in to declared variables*
f. *While loop to fetch next row and loop till no longer rows exist*
g. *Perform any data processing on that row inside while loop*
h. *Close Cursor to gracefully un-lock tables in any*
i. *Remove Cursor from memory*

If the Cursors are called within a stored procedure or a trigger, they can be efficient since there is not network traffic back and forth for fetching of each row and Cursors become part of the same execution plan as stored procedure, which are compiled inside SQL Server, as we saw in earlier Chapter 9.

However, Cursors are generally not recommended due to row-by-row fetching and processing of data, consumption of memory (due to allocation of temporary table and filling it with the result set) and sometimes locking tables in unpredictable ways. Thus, alternate approaches like using *while* loop needs to be considered before using cursors.

### 12.1 LOCAL/GLOBAL CURSOR

This cursor specifies the scope and whether this scope allows locally to a stored procedure or trigger or even a batch OR if the scope of the cursor is applicable globally for the connection. Cursor is valid only within the scope defined.

### 12.2 FORWARD_ONLY CURSOR

*FORWARD_ONLY Cursor* specifies that rows can only be scrolled from first to the end row. Thus, this precludes moving to *prior* or *last* row and *fetch next* is only option available. Below is an example of *FORWARD_ONLY Cursor*:

```
-- =============================================
-- Author:      Neal Gupta
-- Create date: 12/01/2013
-- Description: Create a Cursor for displaying customer info
-- =============================================
DECLARE
    @CustomerID INT
    ,@FirstName VARCHAR(50)
```

```sql
    ,@LastName VARCHAR(50)
    ,@City VARCHAR(50)
    ,@State VARCHAR(10)
    ,@ZipCode VARCHAR(10)

-- Create a Cursor
DECLARE curTblCustomer CURSOR FORWARD_ONLY
FOR
SELECT
    CustomerID, FirstName, LastName, City, [State], ZipCode
FROM [IMS].[dbo].[TblCustomer]
ORDER BY CustomerID ASC;

-- Open the Cursor
OPEN curTblCustomer
-- Get the first Customer
FETCH NEXT FROM curTblCustomer INTO @CustomerID, @FirstName, @LastName,
@City, @State,@ZipCode

PRINT 'Customer Details:'
-- Loop thru all the customers
WHILE @@FETCH_STATUS = 0
    BEGIN
    -- Display customer details
    PRINT CAST(@CustomerID AS VARCHAR(50)) + ' ' + @FirstName + ' ' +
    @LastName + ' '+  @City + ' '+ @State + ' '+  @ZipCode
    -- Get the next customer
    FETCH NEXT FROM curTblCustomer INTO @CustomerID, @FirstName, @LastName,
    @City, @State, @ZipCode
END
-- Close Cursor
CLOSE curTblCustomer
-- Remove Cursor from memory of temp database
DEALLOCATE curTblCustomer
```

Cursor by default is FORWARD_ONLY, if *STATIC, KEYSET* or *DYNAMIC* options are not mentioned and cursor works as a *DYNAMIC* one if these 3 keywords are not specified.

## 12.3 READ_ONLY CURSOR

This cursor is similar to above *FORWARD_ONLY* cursor, except that updates on the current fetched row cannot be performed.

## 12.4 FAST_FORWARD CURSOR

This cursor is really a combination of *FAST_FORWARD* (#1) and *READ_ONLY* (#2) along with performance optimizations. Since, it is a *fast forward* cursor, it precludes scrolling to prior or last row and being *read only* cursor also, prevents update of current fetched row. However, due to these 2 restrictions, they help SQL server to optimize the overall cursor performance.

```
-- ================================================
```

```sql
-- Description: Create a FAST_FORWARD Cursor
===============================================
DECLARE
     @CustomerID INT
    ,@FirstName VARCHAR(50)
    ,@LastName VARCHAR(50)
    ,@City VARCHAR(50)
    ,@State VARCHAR(10)
    ,@ZipCode VARCHAR(10)

-- Create a Cursor
DECLARE curTblCustomer CURSOR FAST_FORWARD
FOR
SELECT
     CustomerID
    ,FirstName
    ,LastName
    ,City
    ,[State]
    ,ZipCode
FROM
    [IMS].[dbo].[TblCustomer]
ORDER BY
    CustomerID ASC;

-- Open the Cursor
OPEN curTblCustomer
-- Get the first Customer
FETCH NEXT FROM curTblCustomer INTO @CustomerID, @FirstName, @LastName,
@City, @State, @ZipCode

PRINT 'Customer Details:'
-- Loop thru all the customers
WHILE @@FETCH_STATUS = 0
    BEGIN
    -- Display customer details
    PRINT CAST(@CustomerID AS VARCHAR(50)) + ' ' + @FirstName + ' ' +
    @LastName + ' '+ @City + ' '+ @State + ' '+  @ZipCode
    -- Get the next customer
    FETCH NEXT FROM curTblCustomer INTO @CustomerID, @FirstName, @LastName,
    @City, @State, @ZipCode
END
-- Close Cursor
CLOSE curTblCustomer
-- Remove Cursor from memory of temp database
DEALLOCATE curTblCustomer
```

## 12.5 STATIC CURSOR

If a cursor is specified as *STATIC*, SQL server takes a snapshot of the data and places into temporary table in *tempdb* database. So, when the cursor fetches next row, data comes from this temporary table and therefore, if something is modified in the original table, it is not reflected in the temporary table. This makes the performance of cursor faster as compared to dynamic cursor (explained below) since next row of data is already pre-fetched in temp database.

## 12.6 DYNAMIC CURSOR

As the name suggests, when the cursor is scrolling to next row, data for that row is dynamically brought from the original table, and if there was any change, it is reflected in the data fetched as well.

## 12.7 SCROLL CURSOR

This cursor allows scrolling of rows: *FIRST, LAST, PRIOR, NEXT* and if a cursor is not specified as SCROLL, it can only perform *FETCH* next row. If the cursor is *FAST_FORWARD, SCROLL* option cannot be used.

## 12.8 OPTIMISTIC/SCROLL_LOCKS CURSOR

This cursor is based on *optimistic concurrency* principle which means that if the data in the table has been modified since the last fetch, and cursor tries to update or delete that data, it will fail, since, the data has already been modified earlier by someone else/other query. It makes sure that the modified data is not over-written or in order words, data is not corrupted by subsequent updates. Alternatively, if we want the update or delete from cursor to always succeed, *SCROLL_LOCKS* can be used which causes SQL Server to lock the row that is fetched into cursor in order to make sure that row is available to be modified by cursor.

Below is a cursor declaration using some of the above options: *LOCAL, FORWARD_ONLY, STATIC and READ_ONLY*:

```
DECLARE curTblCustomerOp1 CURSOR
    LOCAL
    FORWARD_ONLY
    STATIC
    READ_ONLY
FOR
-- Rest of SQL remains same as used in FORWARD_ONLY Cursor
```

Another cursor declaration could use following options: *GLOBAL, SCROLL, DYNAMIC, OPTIMISTIC*:

```
DECLARE curTblCustomerOp2 CURSOR
    GLOBAL      -- OR USE LOCAL
    SCROLL      -- OR USE FORWARD_ONLY
    DYNAMIC     -- OR USE FAST_FORWARD/STATIC/KEYSET
```

```
        OPTIMISTIC -- OR USE READ_ONLY/SCROLL_LOCKS
FOR
-- Rest of SQL remains same as used in FORWARD_ONLY Cursor
```

## 12.8 NESTED CURSOR

As the name suggest, cursors can be nested, meaning one cursor can have another inner cursor and so on. In below example we will use one nested cursor.

```
-- ===============================================
-- Description: Create a Nested Cursor for displaying Orders
-- and products ordered
-- ===============================================
DECLARE
    @OrderID INT
    ,@ProductID INT
    ,@OrderQty INT
    ,@OrderDate DATETIME
    ,@Name VARCHAR(50)
    ,@Manufacturer VARCHAR(50)
    ,@Price DECIMAL(9,2)

PRINT '***** Orders Details *****'

--- First, declare OUTER Cursor
DECLARE curTblOrder CURSOR
    LOCAL
    FORWARD_ONLY
    STATIC
    READ_ONLY
    TYPE_WARNING
FOR
    SELECT
            OrderID
            ,ProductID
            ,OrderQty
            ,OrderDate
    FROM
            [IMS].[dbo].[TblOrder]
    ORDER BY
            OrderID

-- Open OUTER Cursor
OPEN curTblOrder

-- Fetch data from cursor and populate into variables
FETCH NEXT FROM curTblOrder INTO @OrderID, @ProductID, @OrderQty,
@OrderDate

WHILE @@FETCH_STATUS = 0
BEGIN
```

```
      PRINT '*** Order: ' + ' ' + CAST(@OrderID AS VARCHAR(10))


    -- Now, declare INNER Cursor
    DECLARE curTblProduct CURSOR
    FOR
        SELECT Name, Manufacturer, Price
        FROM [IMS].[dbo].[TblProduct] P
        WHERE P.ProductID = @ProductID

    -- Open INNER Cursor
    OPEN curTblProduct

    FETCH NEXT FROM curTblProduct INTO @Name, @Manufacturer, @Price

    -- Loop for INNER Cursor
    WHILE @@FETCH_STATUS = 0
     BEGIN
        PRINT 'Product: ' + @Name + ' ' + @Manufacturer + ' ' +
        CAST(@Price AS VARCHAR(15))
        FETCH NEXT FROM curTblProduct INTO @Name, @Manufacturer, @Price
     END

    -- Close INNER Cursor first and deallocate it from temp database
    CLOSE curTblProduct
    DEALLOCATE curTblProduct

    -- Fetch next Order
    FETCH NEXT FROM curTblOrder INTO @OrderID, @ProductID, @OrderQty,
     @OrderDate
END
-- Finally, close OUTER Cursor and deallocate it from temp database
CLOSE curTblOrder
DEALLOCATE curTblOrder
```

## 12.9 FOR UPDATE CURSOR

This cursor allows updating the column values in the fetched row for the specified columns only, however, if the columns are not specified, then, all the columns can be updated for the row under consideration using *WHERE CURRENT OF* clause.

## 12.10 ALTERNATIVE APPROACH

Note that in above examples, we used cursors to demonstrate the functionality of different types of cursor, however, we could have used alternative approach, like using *WHILE* loop and *counter* approach to perform similar task, as was done in #2 above, as below:

```
-- =================================================
-- Description: Alternative Approach
-- using WHILE loop and Counter Method
-- =================================================
```

```sql
DECLARE @Customers TABLE
(
   RowID INT IDENTITY(1,1) PRIMARY KEY
  ,CustomerID INT
  ,FirstName VARCHAR(50)
  ,LastName VARCHAR(50)
  ,City VARCHAR(50)
  ,[State] VARCHAR(25)
  ,ZipCode VARCHAR(10)
)
DECLARE
       @StartCount INT = 1     -- First Row Count
      ,@EndCount INT           -- Total Row Counts
      ,@CustomerID INT
      ,@FirstName VARCHAR(50)
      ,@LastName VARCHAR(50)
      ,@City VARCHAR(50)
      ,@State VARCHAR(50)
      ,@ZipCode VARCHAR(10)

-- Bulk Insert all the customers into temp table: @Customers
INSERT INTO @Customers (CustomerID,FirstName,LastName,City,[State],ZipCode)
SELECT
       CustomerID
      ,FirstName
      ,LastName
      ,City
      ,[State]
      ,ZipCode
FROM
      [IMS].[dbo].[TblCustomer] WITH (NOLOCK)

-- EndCount is set to total of all rows fetched in above SELECT
SELECT @EndCount = @@ROWCOUNT

-- Loop thru all the rows
WHILE @StartCount <= @EndCount
BEGIN
      SELECT
             @CustomerID = CustomerID
            ,@FirstName = FirstName
            ,@LastName = LastName
            ,@City = City
            ,@State = [State]
            ,@ZipCode = ZipCode
      FROM @Customers
      WHERE
            RowID = @StartCount
```

```
        PRINT 'Fetched Row#: ' + CAST(@StartCount AS VARCHAR(5)) + ' from
        TblCustomer table. Details below: '
        PRINT 'CustomerID = '+ CAST(@CustomerID AS VARCHAR(5)) + '
        FirstName = ' + @FirstName + ' LastName = ' + @LastName + ' City
        = ' + @City + ' State = ' + @State + ' ZipCode = ' + @ZipCode
    SELECT @StartCount += 1
END
```

Hope that this book was helpful to begin your journey to learn SQL Server 2012 with the powerful Management Studio tool.

## APPENDIX A: SQL Standards and Naming Convention

**Naming Convention**: There is a wide variety of opinion regarding naming of various SQL objects. We named customer table as **TblCustomer** where 3 initial letters: **Tbl** represents a table. Reason we choose to follow this naming convention for a table is due to the fact that it is easy to recognize any table in the whole database if it is prefixed with these 3 letters which helps in identifying all the tables, without anyone else having to explain where and what all tables are. If you knew that tables are named with **Tbl**, you will come to associate these 3 initials with a table. Similarly, we will prefix other SQL objects for easy identification.

It is considered a good practice to consistently follow a standard naming convention within a department or even an organization. Every company will typically have their own standard naming conventions and sometimes Gurus debating which one is the best one. It is not important what conventions are followed, *as long as they are followed consistently across the board and by all.* Generally, a development (dev) lead or DBA or Architect or some sr. team member will define these naming conventions for the whole team/department to follow. *It is strongly recommended to have a standard naming convention in place for good coding practices.*

Another good SQL practice for table design is to add following 4 columns in every table. But, for brevity's sake and not to deviate from too much from core task of schema design, adding these 4 columns has been avoided in this book.
1) CreatedBy: Varchar(25), Not-Null, Default value: *System Admin*
2) CreatedOn: DateTime, Not-Null, Default value: GETUTCDATE(): date time in **U**niversal **T**ime **C**oordinated time zone, rather than using date time in local time zone
3) LastUpdatedBy: Varchar(25), Not-Null, Default value: *System Admin*
4) LastUpdatedOn: DateTime, Not-Null, Default value: GETUTCDATE()

## *About Author*

Neal is an Architect, Developer, Technical Evangelist, and writer with more than 15 years of experience in IT field and has worked in top technology companies as well as handled consulting gigs. Neal works on a wide spectrum of Microsoft & Java technologies, since classic ASP, C++/VC++/MFC to when it became ASP.net, C#.Net to open source Java, Beans, and Spring. Neal is a Microsoft Certified Professional (MCP), MCSD.Net with several MS database certifications as well SCJP. Neal also holds a Master's degree in Computer Sc.

Neal would appreciate your feedback to improve this book to help other fellow colleagues and any comments are welcome and can be reached at email address: nealgupta@hotmail.com. Please write SQL Server 2012 in subject of email.

## Dedications:

Neal dedicates this book in memory of his mother Smt. Malti Gupta, a devout and religious person, known for her philanthropy. Also, Neal thanks his lovely wife Amy for her patience and understanding during this project.

Printed in Great Britain
by Amazon.co.uk, Ltd.,
Marston Gate.